INTERNATIONAL
ENERGY AGENCY

SECURITY OF SUPPLY IN ELECTRICITY MARKETS

Evidence and Policy Issues

INTERNATIONAL ENERGY AGENCY
9, rue de la Fédération,
75739 Paris, cedex 15, France

The International Energy Agency (IEA) is an autonomous body which was established in November 1974 within the framework of the Organisation for Economic Co-operation and Development (OECD) to implement an international energy programme.

It carries out a comprehensive programme of energy co-operation among twenty-six* of the OECD's thirty Member countries. The basic aims of the IEA are:

- to maintain and improve systems for coping with oil supply disruptions;
- to promote rational energy policies in a global context through co-operative relations with non-member countries, industry and international organisations;
- to operate a permanent information system on the international oil market;
- to improve the world's energy supply and demand structure by developing alternative energy sources and increasing the efficiency of energy use;
- to assist in the integration of environmental and energy policies.

** IEA Member countries: Australia, Austria, Belgium, Canada, the Czech Republic, Denmark, Finland, France, Germany, Greece, Hungary, Ireland, Italy, Japan, the Republic of Korea, Luxembourg, the Netherlands, New Zealand, Norway, Portugal, Spain, Sweden, Switzerland, Turkey, the United Kingdom, the United States. The European Commission also takes part in the work of the IEA.*

ORGANISATION FOR ECONOMIC CO-OPERATION AND DEVELOPMENT

Pursuant to Article 1 of the Convention signed in Paris on 14th December 1960, and which came into force on 30th September 1961, the Organisation for Economic Co-operation and Development (OECD) shall promote policies designed:

- to achieve the highest sustainable economic growth and employment and a rising standard of living in Member countries, while maintaining financial stability, and thus to contribute to the development of the world economy;
- to contribute to sound economic expansion in Member as well as non-member countries in the process of economic development; and
- to contribute to the expansion of world trade on a multilateral, non-discriminatory basis in accordance with international obligations.

The original Member countries of the OECD are Austria, Belgium, Canada, Denmark, France, Germany, Greece, Iceland, Ireland, Italy, Luxembourg, the Netherlands, Norway, Portugal, Spain, Sweden, Switzerland, Turkey, the United Kingdom and the United States. The following countries became Members subsequently through accession at the dates indicated hereafter: Japan (28th April 1964), Finland (28th January 1969), Australia (7th June 1971), New Zealand (29th May 1973), Mexico (18th May 1994), the Czech Republic (21st December 1995), Hungary (7th May 1996), Poland (22nd November 1996), the Republic of Korea (12th December 1996) and Slovakia (28th September 2000). The Commission of the European Communities takes part in the work of the OECD (Article 13 of the OECD Convention).

FOREWORD

Electricity markets are being reformed around the world. Most OECD Member countries have already introduced competition into their electricity systems and are increasingly allowing market forces to play a role in the development and operation of electricity supply. The main goal of electricity market reforms is to improve the economic performance of the supply industry, but other goals, such as security of supply, remain essential.

Energy security for the electricity sector requires adequate and timely investment in generation and network infrastructures. Markets are a powerful tool for achieving this goal efficiently. Yet the ability of competitive markets to deliver investment in power generation capacity has been intensely debated in the aftermath of the California power crisis. Fortunately, experience in other markets has been more positive.

This book surveys the international experience and confirms that electricity markets are generally working satisfactorily. It also identifies some areas, including the further development of transmission networks, where more investment will be needed to eliminate bottlenecks, facilitate trade and, ultimately, reinforce reliability. Governments play a key role in ensuring the adequate performance of the new electricity markets. Our analysis suggests that, for reforms to work effectively, a new, solid and workable regulatory framework is required, especially for the transition. Although the ultimate objective is a self-sustaining, competitive market, deregulation has proved to be a misnomer for the liberalisation process. Well-designed re-regulation is necessary.

The authors of this book are Carlos Ocaña and Aurélie Hariton. Comments and suggestions from John Paffenbanger, Richard Green, Ignacio Pérez-Arriaga, Jean-Marie Chevallier and various delegates to the Standing Group on Long Term Co-operation are gratefully acknowledged.

This book is published under my authority as Executive Director of the International Energy Agency.

Robert Priddle
Executive Director

TABLE OF CONTENTS

LIST OF FIGURES

LIST OF TABLES

INTRODUCTION

Adequate investment is the key to a secure supply of power

In the long term, the security of electricity supply[1] depends on the adequacy of investment in terms of providing:

- enough generating capacity to meet demand;
- an adequate portfolio of technologies to deal with variations in the availability of input fuels, and
- adequate transmission and distribution networks to transport electricity.

Ensuring a secure electricity supply is an important policy objective in virtually all modern economies. Some of electricity's uses are essential components of modern life. There are limited possibilities for replacing electricity by other forms of energy. Thus underinvestment in the electricity industry is potentially very costly and disruptive.

The investment framework radically changes with market reforms

The reform of the electricity supply industry has profound implications for investment decisions. In the traditional approach to regulation, in which government entities have a direct role in investment, priority is given to ensuring that there is enough capacity to cover demand for power at all times. Costs are also considered, but only to the extent that the ability to meet demand is not compromised. In this context, over the last 20 or 30 years, the electricity systems of most OECD countries have maintained

1. Security of supply refers to the likelihood that energy will be supplied without disruptions. Note that economic variables such as price levels and price volatility are excluded from the definition. However, economic variables generally reflect the state of energy security. Low reliability usually contributes to high and volatile prices.

plenty of assets to meet demand. Security of electricity supply has been consistently high. This approach has also resulted in overinvestment and additional costs to the consumers. In a liberalised market, investment decisions are made by market players who will bear the costs and risks of their decisions. This change generally eliminates the incentives to overinvest that exist in the traditional approach. It is intended to produce a leaner, but still reliable, electricity system.

Most electricity markets contain a number of imperfections and distortions that could have a negative impact on security of supply. Limited demand side sensitivity to market conditions aggravates capacity shortages during peak-demand periods. Price distortions caused by a number of factors may render some investments, such as those on peaking and back-up capacity, unattractive. Policy barriers to the development of certain technologies and to the use of certain fuels may discourage investment. In some particular cases, stringent regulations and cumbersome licensing processes, may deter investors. Since liberalised electricity markets are rather new, relatively little is known about the practical relevance of these potential problems.

The California power crisis and other events have put the spotlight on the investment performance of liberalised electricity markets

This book considers the implications of the new investment framework for security of supply. Public awareness of the potential impact of reforms dramatically increased following the electricity crisis in California in 2000-2001. The crisis resulted largely from a lack of investment in new generation and transmission capacity in the years preceding it. Along with the risks of supply disruptions, discussions on investment in electricity markets also concentrate on the economic implications of low reserve margins – such as the high and volatile prices observed in some markets. Energy markets perform poorly when reserves are low.

The security of electricity supply also depends on the portfolio of technologies used to produce power. The rapid expansion of gas-fired generation in the UK and elsewhere, increased dependence on gas imports in the EU and plans to phase out nuclear and coal generation in several OECD countries have fuelled a debate on the impact of liberalisation on the generation-technology mix.

Key Messages

In summary, this book develops three ideas:

First, energy security requires adequate and timely investment in the energy infrastructure. Markets are a powerful tool to this end. Electricity markets seem to be able to attract investment in generation capacity and to sustain reliability. Electricity prices are key drivers of investment activity. High prices attract investment while low prices discourage it. A debate continues, however, as to whether market price signals are strong enough to stimulate adequate and timely investment, particularly in peaking capacity.

Second, some strategic aspects of security of supply remain within the realm of public policy, including the need for a diversified energy supply and the regulation of those parts of the infrastructure which remain monopolistic. Ensuring adequate investment in transmission networks is a challenge for regulators and policy-makers. The amounts required to reinforce transmission links and to adequately maintain the networks are not large in comparison to the size of total investments in the industry. Augmenting electricity networks is, however, difficult due to site and permit issues. Incumbent companies may have little incentive to invest, since improved transmission capacity may bring increased competition to the areas under their control. There is a need for policies to encourage investment in transmission in many OECD regions in which there is significant congestion of transmission lines, particularly in the links between previously separated electricity systems. Existing interconnection capacity is insufficient in Australia, the EU, Japan and North America. Investments in maintenance and modernisation of the network are also needed regularly. It is important that the increasing pressure on the transmission companies to reduce costs does not reduce reliability.

Third, effective electricity markets do not develop overnight and a sustained government effort is needed during the transition to liberalised markets to monitor reliability, adapt policies and regulations to the needs of an open electricity market and, ultimately, ensure energy security. A key task for governments is to ensure that policies and regulations provide an adequate framework for investment. This task includes minimising distortions to price signals, providing a predictable and stable investment framework, minimising regulatory risk and ensuring consistency among the growing number of policies and regulations that affect ESI investments.

Promoting an adequate investment framework need not conflict with firm policies to promote and protect health, safety and the environment. Most developed countries have such policies and market players seem able to cope with them. Nevertheless, there is often scope to improve the investment framework. The burden of policies and regulations on market players can frequently be reduced through simplification and streamlining of norms and procedures.

Some warnings: the bigger challenges still lie ahead

The condition of most electricity markets before reform was one of comfortable reserves and sluggish demand growth, with the notable exception of California. This provided a cushion against security risks. For some markets, such as the Australian NEM and the Nordic NordPool, it is only now that a real investment challenge has developed as a result of demand growth and other factors.

Despite the globalisation of the world economy, electricity markets remain local. As California's energy crisis showed, reliability varies from one area to the next and over the peaks and troughs of the business cycle. Specific electricity systems face specific risks -the more so, the more isolated they are. Thus, differing performances are likely to continue, reflecting differences in government policies and industry fundamentals.

BACKGROUND: ISSUES, TRENDS AND POLICIES

Investment Decisions: a Primer

A Benchmark: What is Optimal Investment?

There is, at least conceptually, an optimal scale of investment and an optimal technology mix for each electricity system. The optimal investment in electricity generation depends on the value that consumers attach to an uninterrupted supply of electricity. This valuation, known as the Value of Lost Load or VOLL, is defined for each consumer as the monetary value that she or he attaches to the last unit of energy consumed. In other words, VOLL measures how much a consumer would be willing to pay in exchange for not having to reduce his energy consumption by one unit. System VOLL is the VOLL of the consumer with the largest valuation. Estimates of system VOLL range in the order of $ 10,000/MWh. Investment should take place up to the point where cost equals or exceeds VOLL, that is, investment is desirable up to the point where it costs more to expand capacity than the value consumers attach to it. Calculating the optimal investment in practice is, however, very difficult. Box 1 discusses the measurement of reliability in electricity supply.

Investment Under Traditional Regulation

Under traditional regulatory regimes, investment decisions are taken, or at least approved, by government. The planning process aims in principle to achieve the optimal investment level characterised above. In practice, this approach focused on meeting forecast growth in the demand for electricity and on replacing plants that were no longer physically operable. Cost-reducing investments were considered optional[2]. As a result, this approach

2. *Jones (1994) describes the investment planning process by the CEGB, the British electric utility until 1989. Utility investment included essential and optional investments, the former being related to security of supply while the latter concerned cost-minimisation.*

Box 1

Measuring Reliability through Reserve Margins

The reliability of a system depends on many interrelated factors. One synthetic measure often used as a proxy for the reliability of an electricity system is the "reserve margin". It is defined as the percentage of installed capacity in excess of peak demand over a given period (e.g. a year, a semester or a day):

$$\frac{\text{Installed capacity - Peak Demand}}{\text{Installed Capacity}}$$

Installed capacity refers to the generation assets located within a given geographical area but can be adjusted in a number of ways. For instance, import transmission capacity may be added. Unavailable capacity due to maintenance and equipment failure may be discounted. Hydropower capacity may be adjusted downward to account for (fluctuating) water reserves. Peak demand may be adjusted downwards to account for interruptible demand.

A reserve margins approach is used in this book. However, the reader must be aware of the limits inherent to any simple measure of reliability. Factors such as the age and condition of the assets, and the availability of input fuels and imports must also be taken into account in assessing the reliability of electricity systems.

has provided in practice high reliability levels but also resulted in overinvestment.

A number of features of traditional regulation encourage overinvestment, that is, investment over the optimal level discussed above. Traditional regulation passes investment costs on to consumers so that investors are protected against losses arising from overinvestment. Under traditional cost-of-service regulation, there is an incentive to choose too much capital relative to other inputs[3]. At a political level, there is an asymmetry in the consequences of forecasting errors. Blackouts and other consequences of underinvestment are highly visible and may carry substantial penalties for regulators and policy makers. Overinvestment, on the other hand, is less visible and may not be politically penalised.

■ Investment in a Market Setting

Markets can eliminate incentives to overspend. In a liberalised market, electricity prices are the key driver of investment decisions, as they signal potential rewards to investors. High prices relative to the cost of building new generation signal that capacity is scarce and provide an incentive to built it. Low prices discourage investment. Since capacity needs vary with demand, price signals will fluctuate over time. Large spikes in the price of electricity may be required during peak demand periods.

Problems in the Investment Performance of Electricity Markets

A number of market and regulatory imperfections may lead to underivestment and cyclical capacity fluctuations in electricity markets. Price signals may be distorted. High risk may discourage investments if risk hedging instruments are not sufficiently developed. Investment and prices may go through the same kind of cycles that occur in other markets. And regulatory risk may deter investment. Some electrical systems may face special difficulties due, for instance, to the long cyclical variations of water

3. This bias occurs because capital expending is rewarded with a return allowance and is known as the Averch-Johnson effect. If regulators are aware of this bias the investment review process can be used to correct the problem. The result could be a bias in the opposite direction (under investment); this is known as the "reverse Averch-Johnson effect".

reserves for hydropower. Any of these market imperfections could, under certain circumstances, result in low reliability. The relevant question is not whether these imperfections could materialise – the answer is obviously yes – but whether these could significantly damage reliability.

Electricity Price Distortions

In most electricity markets, large categories of consumers are sheltered from market prices and, therefore, do not react to market conditions. For instance, they do not reduce consumption when prices are high. Price caps have been introduced in some markets to compensate for insufficient demand side exposure to market prices that could result in extremely high prices. Price caps are also intended to limit opportunities for the exercise of market power that would result in high prices. Ideally price caps should be set at VOLL, with the aim of mimicking the performance of a competitive market. But VOLL is notoriously difficult to estimate.

If price caps are set too low relative to VOLL the result may be under-investment, particularly in peaking capacity. Other types of price distortions, particularly high prices resulting from oligopolistic market conditions, are not generally a threat to reliability, though they may result in inefficiencies.

Inadequate Risk Management Tools

The insufficient development of risk-management tools may discourage investment. Investments in reserve capacity that is required only rarely may not take place if there are no appropriate instruments to hedge the risk of a very volatile stream of revenues. As an example, rainfall patterns in Brazil and Colombia may require reserves that are not to be used for several years but are essential in dry years. These are, of course, extreme cases. Investment in highly capital intensive technologies with very long amortisation periods, such as some hydropower facilities, may not be undertaken by investors in an open market because of the large risk premiums attached to them.

Efficient risk management may also be made difficult by regulations. A regulated tariff, for instance, may discourage consumers from entering into long term contracts to ensure reliability.

■ Investment Cycles

Cyclical market performance with booms and busts in investment as well as ups and downs in prices has been observed in some industries, notably building construction. It has been argued that cycles could also develop in the electricity industry either as a reflection of the business cycle or as a result of myopic investment decisions[4]. A lag in the adjustment of generating capacity to changing demand conditions could result in periods of low reserves followed by periods of excess capacity. Capacity mechanisms, discussed below, are often proposed as a means to smooth out investment and prices over time.

■ Regulatory Risk

The move toward competition could result in higher-than-normal uncertainty about the shape of reform and future market operation. Such risk may delay or make it more costly to finance investments. Regulatory risk is a major concern for a company which makes a sunk cost investment, as it may fall victim to opportunism on the part of a future regulator – the so-called 'hold up' problem which leads to sub-optimal investment.

---

4. As an example of the 'boom and bust' argument, Ford (1999 and 2000) conducts a simulation of power plant construction in the Western US States, notably California. He argues that cycles could emerge in competitive power markets, mainly because of 'the inherently unstable interactions between the power exchange and investors'. *His simulation yields cyclical variations in the spot price for electricity and in reserves. 'Boom and bust' is primarily due to the fact that investors rely on their own imperfect estimates of future prices combined with delays in the approval and construction of plants. In this model, cycles could be substantially dampened by introducing a capacity payment alongside of the price for energy.*

Regulatory risk encompasses two very different types of uncertainty, namely risk at the time reform is announced and carried out and, then, on-going risk of unpredictable regulatory intervention. Both types of uncertainty may affect investment decisions.

Regulatory risk at the time of reform largely depends on the scope of regulatory reform. Regulatory risk at the time of reform is more likely to be high when the industry undergoes substantial changes such as unbundling, divestitures and the creation of new institutions as was the case in California and the UK. On the other hand, risk is likely to be lower when the industry structure is transformed gradually as in Norway, Sweden and the PJM Power Pool in the US.

Ongoing regulatory risk relates to uncertainty about changes in market rules, regulations and energy policies. It may be aggravated by a lack of clarity about the objectives and future direction of regulation and energy policy. Increasing regulatory discretion and increasing regulatory involvement will increase on-going regulatory risk.

Policy Tools: Capacity Mechanisms and Price Caps

Some electricity markets use capacity mechanisms to procure generating reserves above market levels or to stabilise reserves over time. Capacity mechanisms were used in the England & Wales market until 2001. They function in Spain, some markets in the United States (PJM, NEPOOL and NYPP) and several Latin American markets. Most other electricity markets are energy-only markets in which generators are rewarded only for actual energy supplied.

Capacity mechanisms pay generators in exchange for the generator's undertaking to supply electricity if required. In one version of capacity mechanisms the regulator sets a price for capacity and lets the market determine the amount of capacity available. In the other version, the regulator sets the amount of capacity that has to be available and lets the market determine its price. These are known, respectively, as capacity payments and capacity requirements. With a capacity payment, the cost is controlled by the regulator but the amount of reserves is uncertain. When setting a capacity requirement, the regulator controls the reserve level but the cost is uncertain.

Capacity payments may be used alongside price caps to protect consumers against market power. The thinking behind this approach is that, when capacity is paid for separately, there is no need for price spikes to remunerate reserve capacity. The result could be a reduction in price volatility with no change in average prices and reserves[5]. Price caps, nevertheless, are controversial, as they provide incentives for generators to locate outside areas with low caps.

The use of capacity mechanisms in OECD countries is limited. One reason is that there are non-regulated alternatives to capacity mechanisms, including long-term bilateral contracts for electricity supply and financial contracts that help manage price volatility. Another drawback is that capacity mechanisms, in practice, may give generators opportunities to manipulate prices[6]. There may be incentives in the short run for 'gaming' the rules, for instance, by manipulating the availability of plants to increase revenue. Concerns about anticompetitive behaviour are strongest when capacity is tight and system constraints are common. Another practical concern is the interaction among systems with and without capacity mechanisms, which may lead

---

5. Hobbs, Iñón, and Stoft (2001) have argued that combining installed capacity requirements with a price cap can provide effective incentives for system adequacy if used appropriately. They simulate the operation of three different approaches to capacity incentives in order to compare their performance and effects: (i) an energy-only market relying on the pure price spike; (ii) an ICAP market accompanied by a relatively tight cap on energy prices set at US\$1,000/MWh (like in Pennsylvania-New Jersey-Maryland, PJM); and (iii) an operating reserves payment system in which the market operator pays a fixed price per megawatt, together with a higher price cap of US\$1,815/MWh. Their conclusion is that the three mechanism can be equivalent in terms of reserves and averages prices but differ in the level of price volatility. This would suggest that capacity markets, need not raise consumer costs in the long run and can reduce price swings. Vazques, Rivier and Perez-Arriaga (2001) develop a mechanism that explicitly combines an ICAP and a price cap through an option contract.

6. Concerns about manipulation were at the root of the elimination of capacity payments in the UK.

to distortions. A potential shortcoming of capacity mechanisms is that they may discourage innovation and increase pollution by maintaining uneconomic existing power generating capacity.

Trends in IEA Countries

■ Strong Reserves across IEA Countries but also some Significant Variations

Reserve margins are generally high in IEA countries and have remained strong over the last 15 years (See Table 1 and Figure 1) but there are significant differences among countries. As of 1999, Japan and a number of European countries showed reserve levels in the range of 30% to 50%, well in excess of typical engineering

Figure 1

Reserve Margins in IEA Countries, 1985-1999

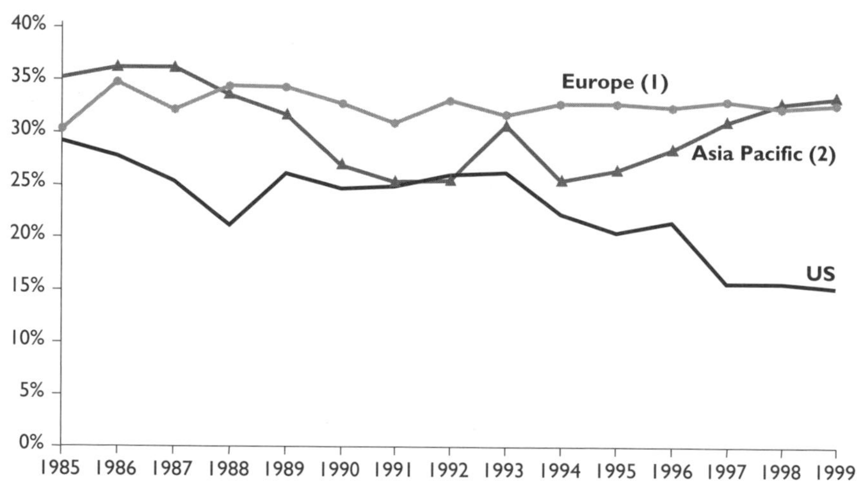

(1) Portugal, Italy, Denmark and the Netherlands not included.
(2) Australia not included.
Source: IEA.

Table 1

Reserve Margins in IEA Countries (%)

	1985	1990	1995	1999
Australia	36	28	-	21*
Austria	-	61 (2)	60	54 (3)
Belgium	38	26	21	18
Canada	26	19	24	-
Denmark	36	36	46	49
Finland	22	23	22	23
France	31	39	38	37
Germany	27	25	28	29
Greece	42	42	32	31
Hungary	6	9	23	26
Ireland	34	32	24	14
Italy	45 (1)	36	40	42
Japan	35	27	26	33
Luxembourg	54	-	-	-
Netherlands	43	39	41	26 (3)
New Zealand	37	29	34	29
Norway	27	37	28	27
Portugal	-	-	52	57
Spain	46	39	44	39
Sweden	27	36	27	23
Switzerland	17	42	42	33
Turkey	40	46	36	34
United Kingdom	21	26	21	23
United States	30	26	20	16

(1)1986 data. (2)1991 data. (3)1998 data. (-) Missing data.

*Source: IEA Database except * taken from ESAA(2001).*

targets for reserves, which are in the order of 18 to 25%. In the US reserve margins have been receding since the mid-1980's and were rather low as of 1999.

A Gradually Changing Fuel Mix

Investment in generating capacity has been strong. Both capacity and generation in IEA countries nearly doubled over the period 1974 to 1999. Capacity growth has been unevenly distributed across technologies (See Figure 2). Investment over the period 1974-1990 was heavily concentrated on nuclear plants and, to a lesser extent, on coal, while oil-fired capacity decreased. Investment in the 1990's largely shifted to gas-fired generation.

Figure 2

Electricity Generation Capacity by Fuel, IEA Total

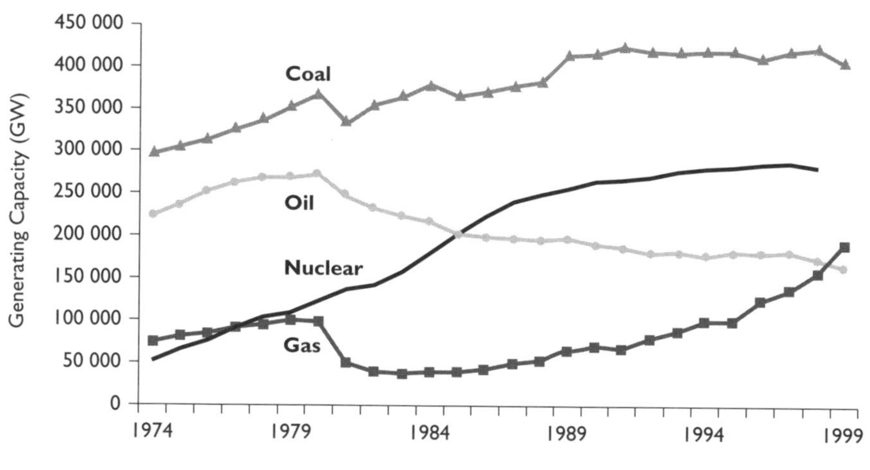

Source: IEA.

These investment trends have resulted in an increase in the share of gas-fired capacity over the period 1985-1999 mostly at the expense of oil-fired capacity, while nuclear has showed a modest increase and hydro capacity has remained stable (See Figure 3).

Figure 3

Generating Capacity Mix, IEA Total

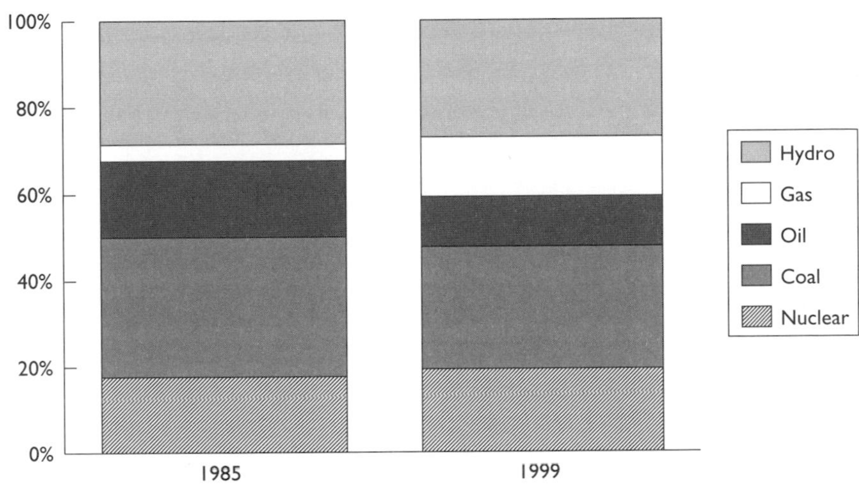

Source: IEA.

GENERATION

This chapter examines the impact of the liberalisation of electricity markets on investment in power generating capacity. It focuses on three issues:

- Investment performance: Is there enough investment to sustain adequate reserve margins? And how is the fuel mix evolving?
- Determinants of investment: What are the main factors affecting investment? Why do investment and reliability differ across markets?
- Role of governments: How do public policies and regulations affect investment? What policies are being used to promote investment and reliability? And what policies may hamper them?

We will seek to answer these questions by examining the performance of six of the early movers in electricity market reform: the UK (England & Wales), Sweden, Norway, Australia and, in the US, California and the Northeast states integrating the PJM Power Pool[7]. We will concentrate on the development of new generating capacity, the evolution of reserve margins and their main determinants and the planning and licensing of generation assets[8]. An overview of investment and security of supply in IEA countries is also provided. Building from the case studies, we assess the performance of electricity markets and briefly consider the role of governments in facilitating a reliable electricity supply. Evidence is still very limited because most electricity markets have been established recently. The assessment below is, therefore, preliminary.

7. *These are Pennsylvania, New Jersey and Maryland.*

8. *There are other related regulations such as environmental, safety, health and land use regulations that are not considered here. These may also have an impact on investment decisions.*

Investment, Reserves and Fuel Mix in Liberalised Markets

Trends in the liberalised markets are not noticeably different from overall IEA trends. Changes in reserves, investment and fuel mix seem to reflect underlying factors such as actual investment needs, the availability of low-cost fuels, and energy policies.

■ A Moderate Decrease in Reserves after Liberalisation

As of 2000, generating reserves have declined in most markets since liberalisation. Only in the case of Australia, where there was significant overcapacity, did reserves drop significantly after reform. In three other cases – the UK, Sweden and PJM – reserves in 2000 were similar to those observed at the time of reform. In Norway there was a decrease of 2% from 1991 to 2000 and, in California, an increase of 1% from 1998 to 2000 was recorded (See Table 2 and figure 4).

Since reserve levels fluctuate over time it is also interesting to compare average reserves in the years before and after liberalisation. As shown in Table 2, average reserves have decreased in all markets examined except for the UK.

The change in reserve margins has occurred in most cases from a starting point of large reserves, so that current reserves generally remain above 16%, which seems acceptable for reliability purposes. Also, in the case of Norway and Sweden, there has been significant integration of the Nordic market which permits a reduction of reserve needs in some areas, particularly in Norway[9]. California, however, is an exception; reserves there were feeble at the time of liberalisation following several years of receding margins, and remained weak from 1998 to 2000.

9. *Because it reduces its high dependency on fluctuating hydro resources.*

Figure 4

Reserve Margins in Selected Power Markets

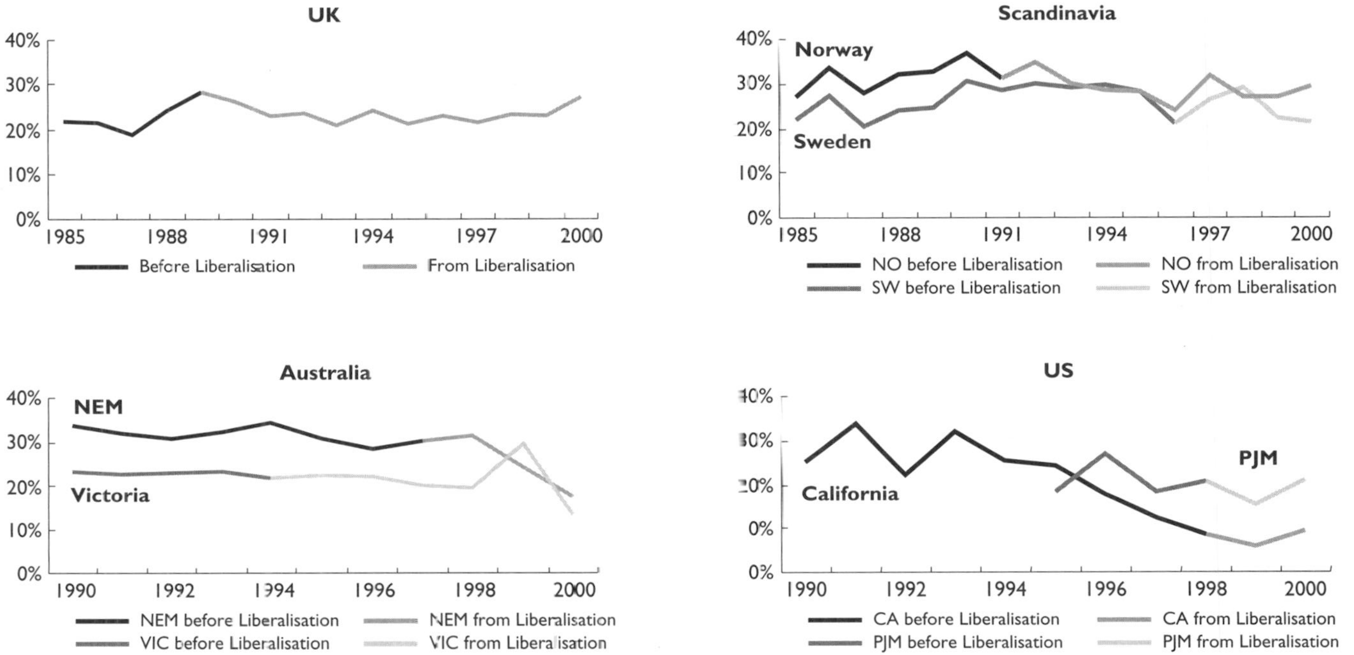

Notes:

- *In PJM, there is approximately 5 per cent interruptible demand which has been included in the reserve margin calculation, for comparative purposes.*
- *VIC means Victoria, Australia.*

Source: IEA.

Table 2

Change in Reserve Margins in the Reformed Markets

	UK	Norway	Sweden	Australia Victoria	Australia N.S. Wales	US: California	US: PJM
Change in reserve margin since year of liberalisation until year 2000	0	-2	0	-24	-13	1	0
Change in average reserve margin(1)	5	-3	-5	-16[2]	-7	-7.5	-3[3]
Year of liberalisation	1990	1991	1996	1994	1997	1998	1998

(1) Difference between average reserves in the five years before liberalisation and average reserves from year of liberalisation to year 2000.

(2) Average four years before liberalization in 1994.

(3) Average three years before liberalization in 1998.

Source: IEA.

■ Investment has Continued

Investment in new capacity has increased net generating capacity since liberalisation in three of the six cases examined: the UK, PJM and Australia's NEM. The increases in generating capacity have, nevertheless, been modest, at levels not exceeding 1.8% per year (See Table 3). Changes in net generating capacity in the other three cases have been very small. These values are in line with those observed in other IEA countries during the 1990s. They reflect moderate demand growth and a starting point of comfortable reserve levels. These figures must be interpreted with care, since capacity additions in any given year result from decisions made several years before and some of the reforms are very recent.

Table 3

Investment Activity in Liberalised Markets
(Annual Change in Generating Capacity up to 2000)

	UK	Norway	Sweden	Australia: NEM	US: California	US: PJM
Average annual change (MW)	585	69	-62	1695	13	573
As % of capacity in 2000	.7	.2	-.2	1.8	.0	1.0
Period since	1990	1991	1996	1997	1998	1998

Source: IEA.

Changes in the Fuel Mix Depend on the Cost and Availability of Input Fuels

The case studies show that changes in the use of natural gas in electricity markets vary by country. This suggest that gas use primarily depends on comparative generating costs and, occasionally, on policies preventing the use of particular fuels. Gas use greatly increased over the 1990's in the UK and California, where alternatives such as coal were uncompetitive on a cost basis. The share of gas in the capacity mix remained low in Australia and PJM, where cheap coal supplies are available. In Norway, the share of gas remained very small as a result of policies against the use of gas in power generation (See Table 4).

This evidence suggests that market competition, per se, does not imply more gas use. Even though the advent of electricity market competition has roughly coincided with a sharp increase in the use of gas in power generation in many countries, in the markets examined the introduction of gas did not take place where low cost coal was available.

Table 4

Growth of Gas-fired Generation (Share of Gas in Fuel Mix, %)

	UK	Norway	Sweden	Victoria	Australia -NEM	California	Pennsylvania
1990	1	0	0.3	12	12	30	0.05
1995	24	0.2	0.5	6(1)	6(1)	31	1
2000	39	0.2	0.2	2	5	38	1

(1) Data for 1996.
Source: IEA.

Role of Prices and Market Structure

A major issue in the deregulation of electricity markets is whether price signals are enough to mobilise investment in a timely fashion. The evidence from OECD markets suggests that investment does indeed respond to prices, but evidence on the timeliness of investments is still inconclusive.

■ Investment Responds to Prices

Economic reasoning suggests that investment in generation should be largely driven by current and expected wholesale electricity prices. Observed patterns are consistent with this expectation (See Table 5). Where prices have been high relative to the cost of building new capacity, investment activity has been vigorous. This has been the case in England & Wales and, over a much shorter period, PJM. California's prices, which peaked in 2000, have also resulted in a surge of investment activity even though this occurred with a lag. Low prices have been followed by weak investment activity in Norway and Sweden. Indeed, in Norway and Sweden most investment has taken place thanks to subsidies given to particular technologies. The situation in Australia's NEM is more complex. There are zones of high and low prices due to the lack of interconnections and transmission constraints between states. The net result has been a significant growth in capacity and a reduction in reserve margins.

Table 5

Wholesale Prices and Entry Costs

	UK: E&W (£/MWh)	Norway (NOK/MWh)	Sweden (NOK/MWh)	Victoria[1] (AU$/MWh)	South Aus[1] (AU$/MWh)	California (US$/MWh)	PJM (2) (US$/MWh)
1990	23						
1991	27						
1992	28						
1993	30	90					
1994	29	180					
1995	27	110					
1996	27	260	250				
1997	27	140	130				
1998	26	120	110	15		30	24
1999	24	110	110	26	54	30	34
2000	24	100	120	29	69	115	31
Indicative range of entry cost[3]	17-20	250-300	250-300	32-40	32-40	27.5-32.4	27.5-32.4

Note: Shaded cells indicate price is below min. indicative entry cost

[1] Fiscal year ending June.

[2] Prices do not include the price of installed capacity.

[3] Based on a variety of sources and IEA estimates. Estimates differ by country according to local conditions

Source: IEA.

Evidence on the Timeliness of Investments is Mixed

The possibility that investment cycles may emerge mimicking "boom and bust" patterns observed in other markets is often cited as a major risk of market liberalisation. Cycles could emerge, for instance, if there were a lag in the adjustment of generating capacity to changing demand conditions. Cycles could represent a major threat to energy security, since periods of low reserves could occur following periods of excess capacity and unsustainable low prices.

There is no conclusive evidence yet on investment cycles and the timeliness of investments. No significant cycles have been observed in, for instance, the UK or Norway after a decade of market operation. On the other hand, the power shortages in California indicate that, under certain conditions, investment may occur too late. The steep downward turn in reserves in Australia also suggests the possibility of a lag in the adjustment of generating capacity to changing demand.

Market Structure Affects Investment

Most electricity markets are oligopolistic to some extent. An oligopolistic market structure tends to favour investment because such structures lead to higher prices and profits thus inducing the entry of new competitors. However, oligopolist companies may also have incentives to deter new entry. Only the UK market has been in operation long enough to allow for an examination of the effects of market structure on investment. In the UK high prices have attracted investment and many new competitors entered the market, thus gradually reducing concentration. Oligopolistic conditions, per se, are not necessarily a barrier to investment and may actually favour it. High ownership concentration, nevertheless, can make it hard to conduct business in otherwise open electricity markets. This has been cited as a problem in Australia, where all generation in some of the states is owned by a single party[10].

10. The issue is discussed in the report of the US IFTC (2000)

Restricted access to fuels, particularly gas, poses a real threat to entry of new players into power generation. Restricted access to gas may occur, for instance, if there is vertical integration into gas of the incumbent electricity suppliers or if there is no effective third party access to gas pipes. These are potentially significant issues in some IEA countries.

Impact of Policies and Regulations on Investment

■ Entry Barriers Arising from Energy Policy Decisions

Barriers to entry resulting from policy decisions, particularly bans or limitations on the use of certain fuels such as gas or hydro, could pose a major challenge to the development of new electricity generation when it is needed. These policies are significant in some countries and may have a large impact in the future even though they have not been a factor in determining investment decisions in any of our six case studies[11].

■ Authorisations

In the California energy crisis, inadequate licensing and siting procedures played a major role in discouraging investment and compromising reliability. With lead times at less than two years for new gas-fired power plants, approval delays of a year or more, and uncertainty about the outcome, added a large implicit cost to the development of new plants. Following the crisis, the authorisation process was reformed leading to a sharp increase in investment levels.

Licensing and siting procedures do not necessarily represent a threat to investment. These are also complex and relatively lengthy in other OECD markets that have showed a satisfactory

11. In Norway and Sweden, for instance, were policy constraints on fuel use are significant, the constraints do not appear to be binding as low prices (reflecting a comfortable supply demand balance) have discouraged investment.

performance. Some degree of complexity and delay is probably inevitable in order to meet safety, health, environmental and other key goals. Much faster and more predictable processes than those in California before the crisis, have been put in place in the other markets examined in this book. Investment has taken place in some of these markets even when strict authorisation requirements were in place. Authorisations are not regarded as a major constraint to investment in these markets.

Regulatory Risk

Regulatory risk can delay or discourage investment. Regulatory risk at the time of reform, resulting from uncertainties regarding the new rules and industry structure is particularly apt to deter investment. High risk could be expected when reform includes an in-depth industry restructuring. The uncertainty that surrounded reforms in California is widely regarded as a leading cause of the state's inadequate investment performance. In Australia and the UK, where changes in the industry structure were also large, no similar problems were reported. Since reserve margins at the time of liberalisation were large in these countries, this could be expected regardless of the level of regulatory risk. In the other cases reviewed in this study, reforms were made with only minor changes to industry structure. This was the case in PJM, Sweden and Norway.

The impact of regulatory risk after reform does not appear to be significant in the cases examined. "Ongoing" regulatory risk seems manageable by investors provided the general direction of reforms and the role of the regulator is sufficiently clear. In the United Kingdom, for instance, investigations into wholesale market operation and other types of intervention have not deterred additions to generation capacity, as the market appeared profitable to investors. Over a shorter time spell, the Australian experience, also punctuated by a number of regulatory reviews, points in the same direction. In PJM, Norway and Sweden, regulatory intervention after reform has been rarer. The California experience was too short to allow for an assessment.

Role of Governments

Role of Governments and Regulators

Governments play a substantial role in determining the framework for investment and monitoring it. There are some uncontroversial roles for governments in a competitive electricity market:

- monitoring with a view to anticipating potential problems;
- setting clear goals and responsibilities for security of supply;
- developing regulation where market forces do not reach, particularly for the networks which remain monopolised;
- minimising regulatory risk and simplifying administration processes;
- ensuring consistency among policies.

There are also other, more controversial actions governments can take, which are only occasionally adopted. These include setting "above market" standards for security of supply, promoting investment through capacity payments, setting price caps, forcing technology choices for power generation and subsidising investment in particular technologies.

Monitoring and Forecasting

Most liberalised markets have established a system to monitor reliability and assess future needs, usually under the responsibility of the system operator and sometimes with the co-operation of other market players as in PJM. This planning and forecasting process provides valuable information to market players and policy makers alike. It may help to counterbalance the uncertainty of the decentralised market setting. The accuracy of forecasts, however, is limited by uncertainty about investment plans in a decentralised market. As an example, applications for licences or even authorisations to build new capacity frequently fail to translate into actual investments.

In some cases, such as the UK and Australia, the monitoring and forecasting function is complemented with an informal consultation process involving the key players. Due to its informal nature, it is difficult to assess the actual contribution of such processes.

In addition to monitoring and forecasting, the system operator, or other designated body, also frequently has a general mandate to act where reliability problems are anticipated. This mandate does not include specific operational rules. In general, the system operator is not expected to play an active role in power generation. There are exceptions, however, as in Sweden, where the transmission company (which is also responsible for system operation) owns some peaking generation units which are used for reliability purposes.

Capacity Mechanisms

There are three basic approaches to the design of electricity markets depending on how capacity is treated. There are energy-only markets, in which capacity reserves are rewarded only for the energy they actually produce. There are energy-and-capacity markets, where an Installed Capacity (ICAP) Market operates in parallel to the energy market. In ICAP markets, an obligation is imposed on suppliers to contract capacity with generators in excess of expected peak demand. This is meant to provide a cushion against unexpected demand and supply fluctuations. It also provides an incentive for generators to invest in reserve capacity. Finally, there are markets that incorporate a capacity payment. In this approach, generators are paid for the capacity they offer to the system at peak hours regardless of whether they actually supply energy or not. The amount to be paid is generally determined by a regulatory decision.

Energy-only markets dominate the scene in OECD countries, the exceptions being some markets in the Northeast of the US where an Installed Capacity market has been established and in Spain, where there is a residual capacity payment in the electricity market. Capacity payments were eliminated in the England & Wales pool in 2001, reflecting concerns about manipulation and doubts about their effectiveness. Outside the OECD, capacity mechanisms have been developed in some South American countries.

Experience with ICAP markets is still limited. There are some design issues that have yet to be solved including their time horizon. The short-term capacity requirements that are currently imposed do not seem satisfactory. Penalties for failing to produce when called upon also need further study. An additional issue is the interaction between systems that have introduced a capacity requirement and systems that have not introduced it.

Price Caps

Price caps have been set in several electricity markets to limit price spikes and prevent the abuse of dominant positions by generators. Even if price caps are set at levels which allow generators to earn a fair return, they may still discourage investment in two ways. If cap levels differ across jurisdictions, generators will have an incentive to locate in high cap areas. Price caps may also decrease incentives for generators to invest in peaking capacity because they eliminate the price spikes that would remunerate them during peak demand periods. The result may be insufficient peaking capacity.

The actual impact of a price cap on investment depends on its level. There is a trade off to be made between protecting users against the abuse of dominant positions and sending accurate price signals to investors. In Australia caps are being raised to AU$ 20,000 to reinforce investment incentives in the wake of reliability problems experienced in February 2000. In California, it was argued that, at certain points during the crisis, a combination of price caps and extremely high gas prices made some generation unprofitable. This was a short-lived issue and its impact on investment was rather minor, but it suggests some of the problems that may arise from capping prices. On the other hand, the "soft caps" imposed by the FERC throughout the Western US and those being considered in Australia, seem unlikely to discourage investment at all.

■ Other Incentives

Other way to ensure adequate incentives and provide reliability would be to impose penalties on supply companies for non-delivery. Unlike ICAP markets and capacity obligations, penalties for non-delivery would come into the play after the fact. So far, this approach is only rarely used. However, if and when bilateral contracts develop, penalties for non-delivery could play a significant role.

A Look Forward

■ How Much Reserve Capacity is Needed?

There is no single figure that defines an optimal reserve margin. Reserve levels in the range of 18 to 25% of total generating capacity are often considered appropriate, but factors such as the size of an electricity system, the degree to which the grid is developed and meshed and the share of hydro in the fuel mix need to be considered in assessing reserve needs for a particular system.

Reserve capacity assessments are further complicated by the integration of previously separated markets in Australia's NEM states, the US, the Nordic countries and the EU as a whole. Reserves are sometimes adequate at the regional level while low in particular areas within the region. There is a debate in some countries as to whether the reference for reliability assessments should be extended to include other countries or states. In the long term, as markets gradually consolidate, an aggregate view is likely to be more accurate. Local "self-sufficiency" goals should be dismissed. However, where interconnections are congested or system dispatch occurs at sub-regional levels, consideration of reserves in particular areas may still be necessary.

■ Increased Flexibility Tends to Reduce Reserve Needs

Reliability criteria may appropriately be relaxed, as the flexibility of electricity systems to respond to a surge in demand increases. Flexibility is increasing as a result of:

- Demand-side measures intended to increase the responsiveness of consumers to supply conditions, such as contracting interruptible load and the introduction of time-of-use pricing. These measures increase the ability of demand to react to a tight supply-demand balance. In addition, increasing consumer awareness[12] of threats to the reliability of this service has proven to be an effective remedy in California, as illustrated in Table 6[13];

Table 6

The Potential of Demand Side Measures: California

Reduction In 2001 Monthly Peak Demand							
	January	February	March	April	May	June	July
Expected Demand MW *	33,743	32,195	32,233	31,888	34,657	39,637	41,599
Actual minus expected demand MW	-2,091	-2,578	-2,967	-2,866	-3,595	-5,570	-4,455
% Demand Reduction	-6.2	-8.0	-9.2	-9.0	-10.4	-14.1	-10.7
Reduction In 2001 Monthly Electricity Use							
Expected Demand MWh *	19,783,184	17,654,385	19,577,401	18,617,765	20,905,847	21,925,523	22,889,024
Actual minus expected demand MWh	-1,067,180	-1,282,347	-1,754,894	-1,276,222	-2,289,362	-2,727,904	-1,201,381
% Demand Reduction	-5.4	-7.3	-9.0	-6.9	-11.0	-12.4	-5.2

(*) Forecast demand adjusted for actual weather and growth
Source: California ISO

12. *Two factors contributed to increase public awareness. First, there were blackouts. Second, there was a steep increase in the price of electricity paid by end-users.*
13. *On the potential and advantages of demand-side measures in expanding generating capacity see also the report of the taskforce on Security of Electricity Supply (Government of Victoria, 2001)*

- The gradual development of bilateral electricity trade. Bilateral trade allows for an increasing differentiation of the reliability needs of each consumer and the price paid for it. This process, however, is of limited importance for domestic and other small end users;
- The deployment of distributed generation and increasing awareness of the existence of large distributed and unused reserves, such as back-up generation. These plants provide additional means to cope with demand peaks;
- The integration of markets. This allows for the pooling of previously separated reserves, reducing reserve needs. Savings from the pooling of reserves can be significant for small systems, but eventually reach a limit.

Improved Market Design and Policy Tools can Reinforce the Investment Framework

There are potential measures –some involving more regulation and some involving eliminating existing regulations– available to improve market design and to counter potential market failures. Price distortions, for instance, can be countered by letting markets determine prices, extending time-of-use pricing and encouraging demand-side participation. Risk and cyclical fluctuations can be alleviated through regulatory measures such as Capacity Mechanisms.

Reliability can be increased by means of regulation, but this comes at the cost of setting up relatively complex regulatory structures. It runs the risk of distorting markets and possibly increasing prices. Reliability can also be increased by improving market mechanisms so that prices better reflect supply and demand.

Box 2

Indicators of Performance of Liberalised Electricity Markets

Despite the newness of electricity market competition, a few studies have already attempted to compile evidence on their performance. These include:

The OECD regulatory database, which has been used by Steiner (2000) to assess the impact of liberalisation and privatisation on the generation segment of the electricity supply industry in 19 OECD countries from 1986 to 1996. The primary findings are that, while changes in legal rules may be slow to translate into changes in conduct, unbundling of generation, private ownership, expanded access to transmission networks, and the introduction of electricity markets affect performance in a statistically significant way.

The study Energy Liberalisation Indicators in Europe (OXERA, 2000) develops a set of indicators to assess the strengths and weaknesses of European countries' liberalisation strategies. Preliminary results suggest that progress is being made towards full liberalisation under the European Union directives, although at variable paces.

The Retail Energy Deregulation Index (RED Index) published by the Center for the Advancement of Energy Markets (2001) describes the movement of states toward competitive electric markets in the United States and Canada. The RED Index measures states' progress in adopting policies that allow consumers to choose their electricity supplier.

TRANSMISSION

Introduction

■ A bottleneck for the electricity supply industry

Despite its small share in the cost of electricity, transmission has become a bottleneck for the electricity supply industry (ESI). Transmission lines are increasingly congested in many OECD countries. Networks are not well adapted to the emerging patterns of electricity transmission. The onset of competition and the gradual regionalisation of markets have led to a sharp increase in cross border and inter-system electricity trade. Existing links, cannot accommodate these new trade patterns. In areas of strong economic growth, transmission within systems is also increasingly congested.

Congested transmission lines have large negative effects. Electricity prices are higher and much more volatile within constrained zones. The cost of supplying electricity increases, since power from low-cost generation sources may be unavailable where it is needed. Competition is hamstrung in the geographically fragmented markets that result from a congested network. A congested network constitutes a major difficulty in the reform of electricity markets. Where transmission lines are used to provide a back up for energy supply, congestion renders supply less reliable.

In the longer term, a congested network can affect the development of new generation capacity. Congestion encourages the development of distributed generation. Distributed generation allows end-users to bypass the network and therefore provides an alternative to developing transmission infrastructure. It brings the benefit of increased reliability but may increase costs when compared to what could be achievable by investing in network development[14].

14. The environmental impact of building more distributed generation rather than expanding transmmission is unclear. It depends on local conditions, such as which distributed resources are developed and which centralised resources are displaced.

Examples abound. Episodes of price volatility and non-reliability in California and other US markets arose, in part, from insufficient transmission capacity during peak demand periods. Limited import capacity has contributed to supply disruptions in, for example,Victoria (Australia) and Spain. In the EU, the development of the internal electricity market is limited by the capacity of existing interconnectors; there are four or more differentiated electricity trade areas (the Nordic region, the UK, the Iberian peninsula and the remaining continental EU)[15]. In Australia, stronger inter-regional links are needed for the development of competition in the National Electricity Market. In Japan, limited interconnections across the networks owned by vertically-integrated utilities constrain competition.

Additional investment is needed, but building new lines is difficult

Additional investment in transmission is necessary to reduce the congestion of transmission lines. But building new lines is becoming increasingly difficult. Investment in many OECD countries is subject to stringent siting and environmental criteria and is sometimes challenged by local groups. Technical solutions, such as underground lines, exist to meet these challenges but they are often prohibitively expensive.

Increasing transmission capacity across national, state and system borders is particularly challenging. Incumbent utilities, to the extent that they remain vertically integrated, may lack incentives to increase interconnections. Building crossborder links can also require agreement between countries with different regulatory regimes[16].

Implications for policy

Under current policies, the development of transmission networks in most OECD countries will proceed slowly. Additional

15. *Plus Greece and Ireland, which are not interconnected to the rest of the EU.*

16. *See Newbery (2002).*

transmission capacity will be procured mostly by upgrading existing lines. Congestion will remain or increase. In order to counter this trend, higher priority should be given to developing transmission links. Specific policy actions can improve the outlook for transmission development.

OECD countries are increasingly aware of the need to reinforce and reform transmission systems and are considering measures to deal with it. The new "National Energy Policy" proposed in the US[17], and the proposals of the EU Commission on "European energy infrastructure"[18] are two examples. These initiatives aim to maintain the security of electricity supply, to reduce the cost of electricity supply and to facilitate the development of competition.

Governments have a number of tools to promote investment in transmission:

- Legal, administrative and regulatory processes should avoid unnecessary delays and uncertainty in the licensing of new installations. Attention must be given to siting problems, which are often a barrier to the timely development of electricity networks.
- The development of cross-border and inter-system links must be addressed at a high institutional and political level, as it involves different jurisdictions and governments, and requires some degree of harmonisation of the rules concerning their use.
- Alternatives to building new lines must also be considered. Improving existing facilities can provide, in some instances, an inexpensive and acceptable alternative to building new lines. Upgrades increase capacity but not reliability. Complementary measures to promote the development of distributed generation and demand-side measures can also ease transmission constraints.

17. Report of the National Energy Policy Development Group, May 2001 (http://www.whitehouse.gov/energy/). On May 2002, the US Department of Energy made a number of specific recommendations to modernize the US transmission system, including measures to facilitate investment in transmission and promote compliance with reliability standards ("National Transmission Grid Study", US DOE, 8 May 2002).

18. Communication published on 20 December 2001

Implications for the organisation and regulation of transmission activities

The introduction of competition brings with it deep changes in the organisation and regulation of transmission activities. These may include the unbundling of transmission, the introduction of incentive regulation for transmission activities, the development of new transmission-pricing methods and the harmonisation of regulations across countries and states. Reforms typically result in more, not less, regulation of transmission activities. The role of market mechanisms in transmission is bound to remain limited, due to the monopolistic nature of electricity networks and interdependencies between transmission and generation. The box below summarises the main characteristics of transmission.

While the main reason for these regulatory changes is to make competition possible, sustaining adequate investment and reliability is also necessary. The regulatory framework must provide robust incentives to invest and must define clear responsibilities for planning, development and monitoring of transmission. This has some important implications for the design of regulation.

First, the roles of the various players involved in transmission – system operators, transmission companies, intersystem reliability organisations[19], regulatory agencies, etc. – have to be clearly and consistently defined. Designing effective structures for their management can be difficult due to the complex organisational architecture of some transmission systems. In addition, the geographical scope of transmission entities needs to be reviewed in light of the development of regional markets. Regionalisation requires greater coordination or integration among system operators and transmission companies. Reliability, too, has to be considered in the larger context of regional markets and intersystem reliability organisations have to be adapted accordingly.

---

19. Such as the North American Electricity Reliability Council (NERC)

Box 3

Transmission Networks Defined

Transmission refers to the transportation of electricity over an interconnected network. In practice it refers to the transportation of electricity at very high voltage levels, typically 115 kV and above or 220 kV and above. The function of transmission is to co-ordinate the supply of electricity. Co-ordination reduces the cost of generating electricity by using the lowest-cost electricity available. It also increases the reliability of supply by pooling generation reserves. The share of transmission in total electricity costs is small, from 5 to 10%, and depends on geographical factors and utilisation.

Transmission includes several activities such as construction and maintenance of transmission lines and system operation. System operation is the co-ordination of transportation services to ensure that the system is constantly in a state of electrical equilibrium. Equilibrium requires that power supplied equals power demanded at each node of the network. This state is achieved by controlling inflows and outflows of energy over the entire network and by procuring the complementary services necessary to maintain the technical reliability of the grid. Regardless of the market framework, system operation is always a monopoly. Interconnection, with the associated benefits of increased reliability and lower costs, is possible only under a centralised system operation. However, transmission lines within the grid are not, in general, natural monopolies. Two transmission lines may run more or less in parallel and still be economical.

The transmission network has some special characteristics. There are economies of scale both at the single line level and system-wide; there is, therefore, a minimum efficient scale for transmission lines and transmission systems. The value of investments in transmission assets depends on investments made in other transmission and generation assets. The value of investments in grid augmentation, for instance, may be reduced by successive investments in generation that make the additional transmission capacity unnecessary. This so-called "network externalities" may discourage investment.

Figure 5

Cost Shares of Electricity Supply

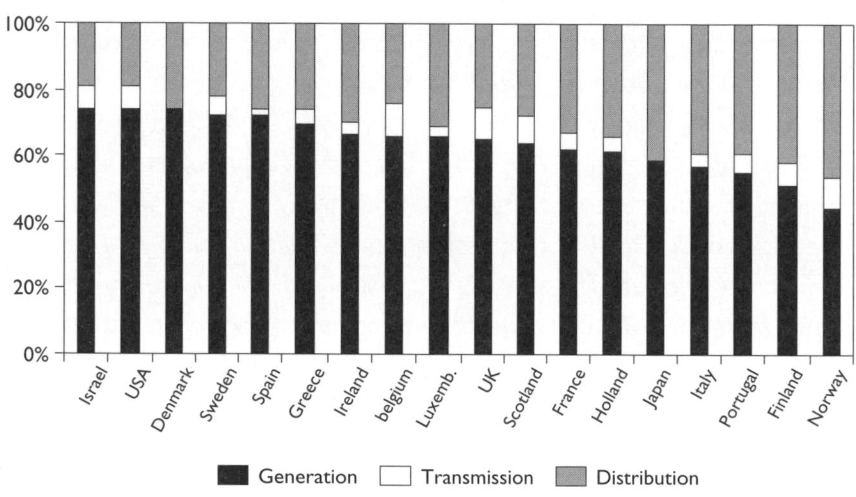

Source: IEA.

Figure 6

Electricity Exports (Billion kWh)

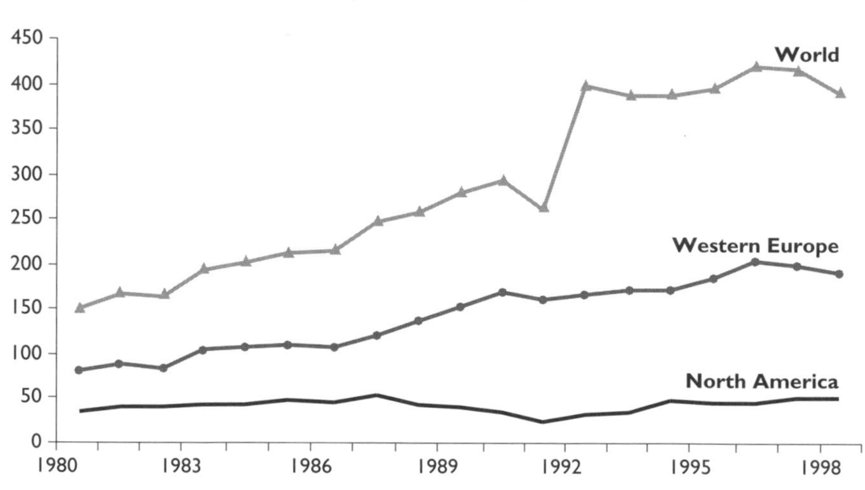

Source: Energy Information Administration (DOE, US).

Second, transmission activities have to be financially sustainable. Transmission prices must allow adequate returns to investors and provide sufficient incentives to attract investment where it is needed. Setting efficient transmission tariffs is a complex matter, particularly where the ownership of transmission is fragmented. Pressures to reduce costs should not prevent adequate investment in maintaining and enlarging the grid.

Current Investment Needs

■ Overview

Transmission networks are highly developed in most OECD countries. In the wake of several technological advances, the transmission networks of industrial countries were greatly expanded during the 1960's, 1970's and 1980's. Investment in transmission has decreased in recent years reflecting smaller needs and greater difficulty in getting approval for new lines. No major capacity additions are currently planned in the US, for instance[20].

There are three areas in which more investment in transmission is required:

- There is scope for stronger links between electricity systems. Existing transmission networks were primarily designed to serve single electricity systems. They cover a country or, in large federal countries like the US, Germany, Canada and Australia, a region within the country. Interconnections between systems are less developed[21]. Interconnectors were usually intended to increase system reliability and reduce blackouts, but not to accommodate high volumes of trade. Existing interconnection capacity is scarce in most OECD regions, including Australia, Europe, Japan and North America.

20. *The length of the lines over 230kV is expected to grow by only 3.7% from 1999 to 2008 according to NERC 1999 Reliability Assessment.*

21. *There are exceptions, as in the Nordic countries, where strong interconnections between national systems do exist.*

- Investment within transmission systems is needed in some high economic growth areas such as Ireland and California.
- Maintenance and modernisation of the network is needed regularly. This requirement can be expected to increase as transmission assets grow older. This is an issue that deserves monitoring, even if the amounts involved are not very large, to ensure that increasing pressure on transmission companies to reduce costs does not reduce the reliability of electricity supply.

■ Australia

Interconnections between regions in Australia are not strong, and some states are isolated from the rest of the nation. Interconnections between the regions of the National Electricity Market (NEM), as shown in figure 3, are scarce relative to a generating capacity of nearly 31,400 MW. Isolated systems remain in Tasmania, Western Australia and the Northern Territory. Transfer capacity between the five NEM regions is limited; as a result, electricity prices often differ across regions[22]. In February 2000, the state of Victoria experienced a power shortage. This prompted a review of the factors affecting the reliability of the system, including interconnections.

The construction of some additional interconnection capacity to connect South Australia and New South Wales is being considered. There is also a "merchant" interconnector between New South Wales and Queensland ,with a capacity of 180 MW. Three other "merchant" interconnectors are being considered (480 MW between Tasmania and Victoria, 250 MW between Victoria and South Australia and an additional 65 MW between Victoria and South Australia). "Merchant" or unregulated interconnectors earn market rates, so there is no guarantee that investment costs will be recovered. Despite these risks, investment is taking place.

22. *In the absence of transmission constraints, a single price would be set for the five regions.*

Figure 7

Inter-regional Links Between Australian National Electricity Market Regions, 1999

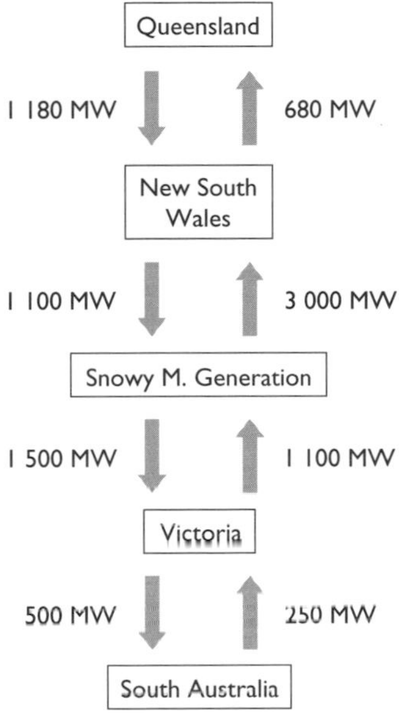

Source: Department of Industry, Science and Resources, Australia.

■ EU

In the European Union, limited interconnections divide the area into at least four differentiated markets, as shown in figure 4. There is a well-interconnected "central" market that accounts for two thirds of EU electricity consumption, including France, Germany, Italy, Belgium, the Netherlands and Austria. The three other markets are in the Nordic countries, the UK and the Iberian peninsula. Within the central market, some links are congested during periods of peak demand. This is the case for Italy, which has congested links with France, Switzerland and Austria, and the Netherlands, which has congested links with Germany and Belgium. The Nordic and UK markets are connected to the central market through direct-current

Figure 8

Market Fragmentation in the EU

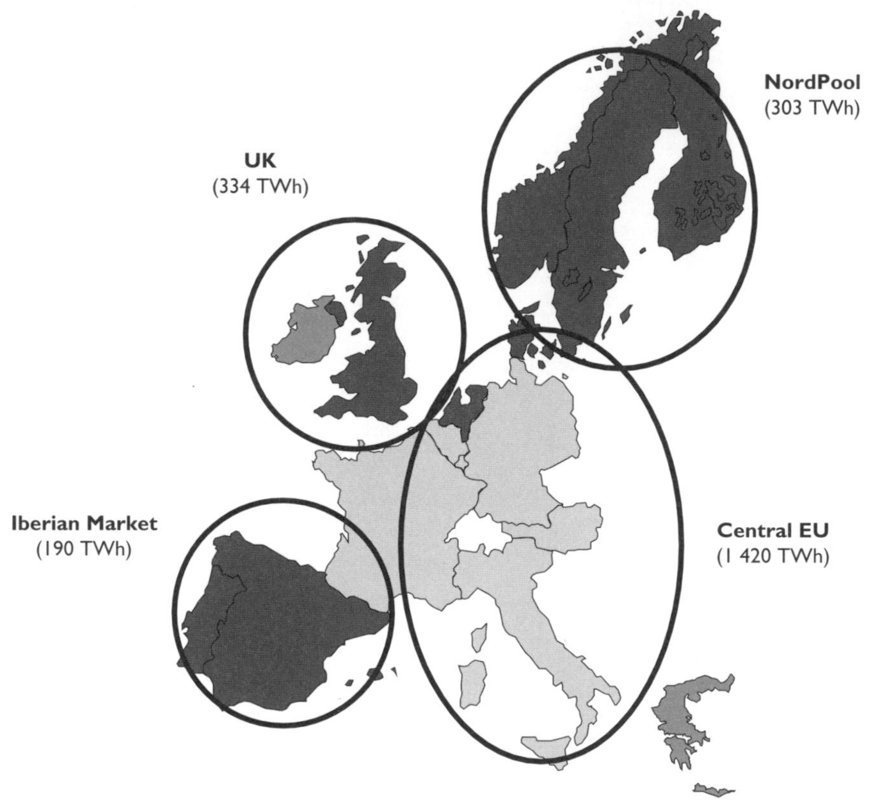

1997 consumption.

Source: IEA.

lines of limited capacity[23]. The links between the Iberian and central markets only provide some 900 MW of commercially available capacity; this amounts to 6 TWh of maximum transfer capacity per year or about 3% of Iberian consumption.

23. With the exception of the Western part of Denmark which belongs to the Nordic market but is linked by AC lines to the central market.

Investment needs in the EU are substantial. The EU commission has identified a number of links whose development is of "common interest" to EU members[24]. These projects include[25]:

- connection of isolated electricity systems: Ireland to Wales, Northern Ireland to Scotland, Greece to Italy, and various islands to the UK and to Greece;
- development of interconnections between member states: Germany-Denmark, France-Belgium, France-Germany, France-Italy, France-Spain, Belgium-Luxembourg, Spain-Portugal, Finland-Sweden, Austria-Italy, Austria-Germany and the Netherlands-UK;
- development of lines within member states to improve use of interconnectors in Denmark, the Netherlands, France, Spain, Italy, Portugal, Greece, Ireland, Sweden, Germany and the UK;
- development of lines with third countries: links to virtually all neighboring countries.

Japan

The utilities serving the eastern part of Japan (Hokkaido, Tohuku and Tokyo) deliver electricity at a frequency of 50 Hertzs. Western Japan uses 60 Hertzs. All four main islands of Japan and the nine electricity generation regions have transmission links, making national inter-regional power exchange possible. Frequency converter stations exist, but total interconnection capacity between the two frequency areas is limited to 900 MW[26]. Transmission links have been upgraded to improve reliability, but are limited by the mountainous terrain and the elongated shape of Japan, which restricts opportunities for enhancing networks through parallel transmission lines. Seven

24. *More details can be found in the "Communication from the Commission to the Council and the European Parliament on European Energy Infrastrucuture", EU Commission, 2001.*

25. *Commission decision defining projects of common interest, COM(2000) 2683 final.*

26. *Source: Electric Power Industry in Japan 1997/98, Japan Electric Power Information Center, Inc., Tokyo, 1997.*

large transmission projects to increase inter-regional links are under construction or have been planned. Okinawa is not connected to the main grid. There is no grid connection between Japan and other countries.

Developing grid interconnections could increase competitive rivalry among the utilities, as existing interconnection capacity reduces the scope for power trading between service areas. For example, if all six utilities in the 60 Hz frequency zone of Japan were in a single electricity-trading region, no utility would have more than 35% of the generating capacity. These potential benefits must be weighed against the relatively high cost of expanding transmission lines in Japan.

Figure 9

Transmission Capacity and Peak-load in Japan (MW)

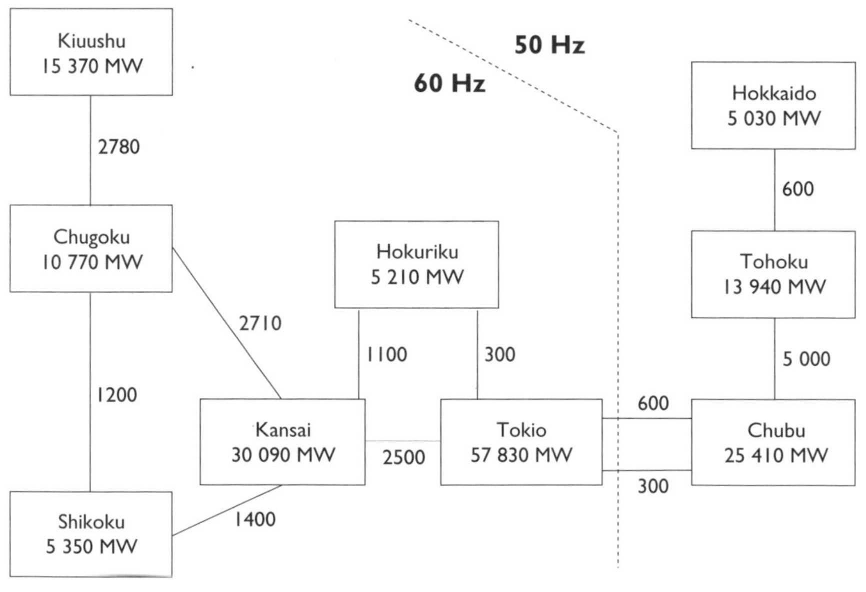

Source: METI.

North America

Figure 6 shows that transmission investment in the North America has decreased in recent years relative to demand growth and is expected to remain weak. The slowdown in investment particularly affects interstate transmission projects. Examples of apparently needed interconnectors that have not been built include expanded interfaces between New York and New England, New York and Pennsylvania-New Jersey-Maryland, Wyoming and Colorado, Indiana and Michigan, Georgia and Florida, and Minnesota and Wisconsin[27].

The use of transmission lines has rapidly increased in recent years, resulting in congestion in many areas. The use of procedures for transmission loading relief – an indicator of transmission capacity nearing its limits – has increased steadily over the last four years and more than doubled during the first nine months of 2000 compared to the previous year. This trend has been particularly intense in the Northeast US, and California. Transmission ties among the three North American interconnections – Eastern, Western and ERCOT (Texas) – provide transfer capacity of only 1,850 MW, 1,080 MW and 856 MW, respectively[28].

Transmission constraints in some regions can give specific companies considerable market power in certain areas. The following are some examples of companies enjoying regional market power[29]: The Southwest Power Pool imports only 5% of total sales and one utility, Entergy, owns 68% of the region's generating capacity and 80% of its peak capacity. Michigan is another pocket of severely constrained interstate electricity trade, partly because it is largely surrounded by the Great Lakes. Here, two big utilities, Detroit Edison and Consumers' Power, virtually control the market. Virginia Power, a utility that supplies an area close to Washington, D. C., is another example of the market

27. *See E. Hirst: "Do We Need More Transmission Capacity?". The Electricity Journal, November 2000.*

28. *Detailed assessments are regularly issued by The North American Electricity Reliability Council, see http://www.nerc.com/.*

29. *Energy Policies of The United States, 1998 Review. IEA*

Growth Rates in Transmission Capacity and Summer Peak Demand

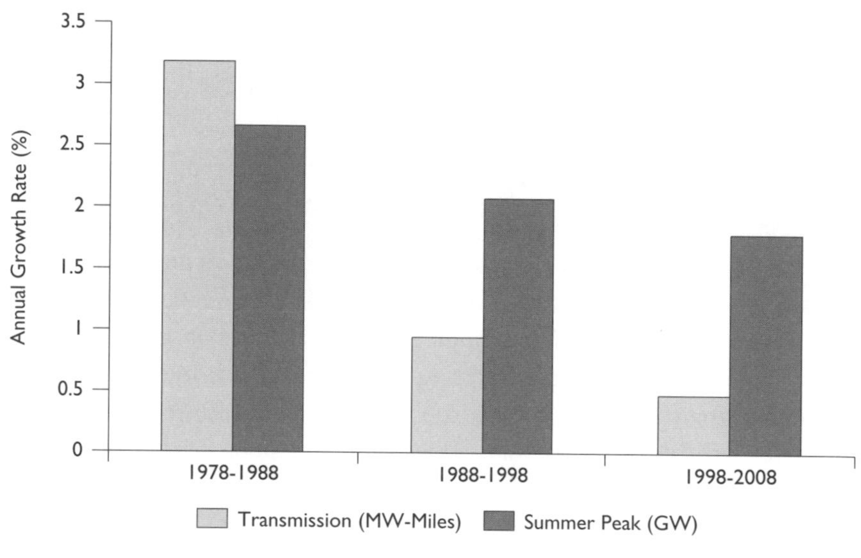

Source: NERC (2000): Reliability Assessment 1999-2008. Adapted from Hirst (2000)[1].

power that transmission constraints can create. The utility has consistently posted "zero available transmission capacity" on the electronic bulletin board for competitive inter-state power trading, thereby keeping competitors out of its market.

Options to Relieve Transmission Congestion

Expanding and Upgrading Transmission

In the long term, adequate investment in transmission assets is the key to an efficient transmission system. Incremental investment in existing networks relieves congestion from transmission lines that are operating at or near their maximum capacity. It also provides a cushion to increase reliability[30]. Investment can be used to build new lines or, when feasible, to upgrade existing ones. Upgrade options include "restringing" – replacing lines with larger ones –, "bundling" – adding more lines to existing structures –, increasing the voltage of transmission and increasing the number of circuits. Investment costs vary by project. Typical costs for a new 230kV line with a capacity rating of about 1,000MW are in the $400,000 to $600,000 range per kilometer. These figures do not include the cost of rights of way, which can be high[31]. Upgrading a line, where feasible, is usually quicker and less complicated than building a new line. On the other hand, upgrades contribute less to the reliability of the system than building new lines. Investment costs are amortised over 25 to 30 years, reflecting the long economic life of transmission assets.

Changing power flows can also alleviate congestion. Improvements in system operation, such as better software and protocols, may allow for a better configuration of power flows. Changes in operating philosophy may allow for a more intense but less reliable use of the network. Transmission capacity constraints may also result from insufficient availability of ancillary services such as reactive power. Easing these technical constraints requires either building new generation units or offering financial incentives for existing generators to provide these services.

Distributed Generation and Demand-side Measures

Congestion in transmission lines can also be relieved by changes in generation and end-user demand. Those making decisions to expand the grid need to consider the feasibility and cost of these alternatives.

---

30. In addition, there are dedicated transmission lines to connect generators and very large consumers to the grid.

31. These figures have been adapted from Fuldner (1998), "Upgrading Transmission Capacity for Wholesale Electricity Trade", http://www.eia.doe.gov/cneaf/pubs_html/feat_trans_capacity/ and reflect US data. Estimates of the cost of upgrades can also be found in this article.

Generation capacity located near consumption centers – distributed generation – is one substitute for transmission as it reduces the need to transport electricity over the transmission network. Distributed generation reduces consumers' dependence on the network, thus increasing reliability. Distributed generation is, in general, more expensive than centralised generation but its cost is falling. Distributed generation used in combination with centralised generation can be cost effective as it can be used at times of peak demand and switched off at other times.

It is unclear whether distributed generation is cost effective compared to augmenting transmission capacity. One study by the California Energy Commission[32] finds that "distributed generation... is probably not capable of providing equal reliability benefits per dollar of investment in a transmission upgrade". In spite of this general assessment, particular distributed generation units can be effective in providing reliability. The study concludes that distributed generation and transmission upgrades should be pursued as a package to improve reliability and reduce costs.

Distributed generation raises new challenges for grid planning, as it has to be incorporated in load forecasts. There is much uncertainty concerning the growth rate of distributed generation and how it will change peak demand. This makes forecasts of transmission needs more uncertain.

Demand measures to reduce transmission needs include time-of-use pricing of electricity and energy efficiency investments. Time-of-use pricing gives consumers incentives to reduce consumption during peak demand periods. It is widely practised for large users in most OECD countries and increasingly for smaller ones. This approach is effective in smoothing out consumption over time and reducing capacity needs. Energy-

32. *"The role of energy efficiency and distributed generation in grid planning", April 2000.*

efficiency investments reduce energy use and thus obviate the need for transmission capacity, but they have no direct impact on reliability. They take place in a highly decentralised fashion and are outside the control of the system operator. Despite these practical limitations, energy efficiency investments are often cost-effective.

■ Policy Measures to Promote Investment

There is a clear need across the OECD to develop electricity networks further and to reinforce cross-border links. Current investment plans are inadequate to meet this need. Congestion is likely to occur during periods of peak demand in many electricity systems. Government policies can help to bridge the gap between investment needs and plans.

The general framework for investment in transmission is a key determinant of investment activity. Procedures for the licensing of assets are complex. They involve technical and environmental-impact assessments, obtaining the necessary rights of way – a process that sometimes involves requisition issues and several overlapping jurisdictions – and regulatory reviews to determine costs. These procedures, while necessary, can impose substantial delays and reduce investment activity. It is thus important to ensure that these procedures are efficiently managed. Red tape should be minimised and so should opportunities for third parties to create unnecessary delays. In the US, for instance, the proposed Electric Power Market Competition and Reliability Act contains measures to facilitate investment in transmission assets and the Federal Energy Regulatory Commission is given the right of eminent domain to build new interstate transmission lines, but this legislation has yet to be passed by Congress.

The general regulatory environment is also important. Regulatory uncertainties linked to ongoing reforms of electricity markets, may delay investment. Large uncertainties may arise, in particular, during the elaboration of new laws and regulations.

Box 4

Technical Background: Relieving Transmission Constraints

When transmission capacity is limited, upgrading existing lines is sometimes a less expensive option than building new ones. Available upgrade options depend on whether transmission capacity is limited by thermal, voltage or system operating constraints.

Overheating reduces the expected life of the line and expands it, creating sags between the supporting towers and reducing clearance from the ground. This is, however, a gradual process that can be accommodated for limited time periods. Thermal constraints can be alleviated by replacing existing lines with larger ones (restringing) or adding more lines to form bundled lines. These approaches usually require reinforcement of the tower structures and enhancing substation equipment. This may be the only feasible alternative but it is usually expensive. There may be other less costly options. It may be possible to increase the transfer capability of the line by monitoring lines in real time and applying modern methods for computing thermal ratings. Since the thermal limit of a transmission line is based on the component that would be the first to overheat, the thermal rating of the line can sometimes be increased by replacing an inexpensive element. Another option is to increase allowable temperatures, which reduces the life of the lines.

Maximum-voltage constraints depend on the design of the transmission line. Exceeding the maximum voltage may result in short circuits, interference and damage to transformers and other equipment. End-user needs also impose minimum voltage constraints. Special devices, such as capacitors and inductive reactors, are installed on the lines to mitigate the drop in voltage that tends to occur as electricity flows from the sending end to the receiving end.

Increasing the operating voltage within a voltage class is an option when the system does not reach the upper voltage limit under normal operation. It requires adjusting the voltages of the generators and

Box 4

Technical Background: Relieving Transmission Constraints (continued)

transformers, or possibly replacing some transformers. Reactive power flows, which are a source of voltage constraints, can be controlled by means of capacitors or reactors placed at strategic locations of the network. Voltage changes to a higher voltage class usually require substantial reconstruction of the transmission lines.

Operating constraints are set by the system operator in order to maintain the power flows in equilibrium and ensure a secure and reliable supply of electricity. Power flows change as a result of changes in demand and generation patterns change. Sometimes, the distribution of power flows through a transmission network can be improved so that the loading on a critical line is reduced. Reconfigurations may require a small investment, such as the addition of some circuit breakers, or no investment (e.g., if the circuit breakers already exist). Power flows can also be altered by introducing some special devices, such as phase-angle regulators, which are relatively costly, a series capacitor or a series reactor.

Operating procedures can also be change to increase transfer capability. The traditional "preventive" approach aims to ensure that no action is required in the event of a contingency other than clearing the fault. Technological improvements are allowing a shift towards a "corrective" operation approach, which requires immediate action, such as switching circuits. Corrective operation is less reliable than preventive operation, but allows greater power transfers during normal operations. Flexible AC Transmission System (FACTS) are increasingly used to increase reliability in this new operational setting. FACTS uses new electronics devices to provide faster and finer controls of equipment

There are additional options that may be applied, in principle, to deal with any type of constraint. These include increasing the number of circuits,

Box 4

Technical Background: Relieving Transmission Constraints (continued)

thus converting single circuit towers to multiple-circuit towers, and converting alternating current (AC) lines to high-voltage direct current (HVDC) lines. HVDC circuits have some advantages over AC circuits for transferring large amounts of power over long distances but are also more expensive.

Source: Upgrading Transmission Capacity for Wholesale Electric Power Trade *by Arthur H. Fuldner. Energy Information Administration (DOE, US).*

Cross-border Interconnections

■ Overview

A large fraction of investment needs for transmission concerns cross-border interconnections. These raise a number of specific issues in addition to those considered in the previous section[33]. Three key issues are:

- the integration of electricity markets and their harmonisation;
- the regulation of interconnectors, particularly concerning access and pricing;
- reliability.

33. These issues are discussed in detail, in the EU context, in "Second report to the Council and the European Parliament on harmonisation requirements", EU Commission, 16 April 1999.

Cross-border interconnectors bring major benefits to electricity systems. Interconnectors improve the reliability of electricity systems and allow for more economical system operation. They reduce the need for reserve and peaking generation capacity and allow more efficient dispatch. The development of interconnectors is also instrumental in improving market performance because it brings competition from generators in other electricity systems.

The development of cross-border trade is also an issue for the natural gas industry. There are some similarities between electricity and gas trade, in that both require the development of cross-border infrastructures. There are, however some differences that make the development of electricity trade somewhat easier. The magnitude of the investments required is much bigger for gas than for electricity. Electricity trade goes in both directions, and so it tends to increase reliability and security of supply. Gas trade normally goes in only one direction and this, in some instances, can raise security of supply concerns.

■ Integration of Markets and Harmonisation

Integrated electricity markets covering several countries or several states within a federal country are now emerging in many OECD regions. This is the case in the EU, the US and Australia. A well functioning regional market requires some degree of harmonisation of the regulations applying in each jurisdiction. A set of common rules or at least a compatible approach is needed on the degree of market opening, network access and other aspects of the regulation of electricity markets. Also, fiscal arrangements affecting market players and environmental regulations need some degree of harmonisation to avoid distorting competition.

Harmonising the regulatory framework is a complex process because it requires the agreement of several independent jurisdictions. Substantial progress has been made in developing regional electricity markets, but much remains to be done. The following examples show how the regionalisation of electricity markets is evolving across OECD countries.

In the EU, the basic framework for electricity trade is contained in the electricity directive and the transit directive. But the directives do not set concrete guidelines for international transmission. An informal body, known as the EU Regulators' Forum, was set up following the implementation of the electricity directive to discuss transmission pricing and related issues. It includes the European Commission, regulators and ministries from member states, and the European Transmission System Operators Association (ETSO). After two years of discussions, the forum has agreed on the general principles, including that prices should be cost reflective, but the discussion remains open on some critical issues such as the tariff level. The issue of investing in additional cross-border transmission capacity has been recognised by the EU Commission as essential to the further development of the market, but mechanisms for financing it have not yet been developed.

In the Nordic region, the electricity markets of Sweden, Norway, Finland and Denmark are highly integrated. Building on a similar regulatory framework in each of the four countries, an international power exchange (NordPool) has operated in Norway and Sweden since 1996, in Finland since 1998, in western part of Denmark since 1999 and in the eastern part of Denmark since 2000. Cross-border transmission tariffs have been abolished and trade across national boundaries is unrestricted. There is close co-operation among system operators through Nordel, the association of Nordic system operators. Nordel deals with system development and rules for network dimensioning, system operation, reliability of operation and exchange of information and pricing of network services. This approach has succeeded in attaining a high degree of harmonisation through informal co-operation.

The Australian National Electricity Market (NEM) provides a successful example of integration of previously separated state electricity markets. This was achieved through co-operation and consensus building among the states, which have ultimate responsibility for many aspects of electricity regulation. The federal government played a key role in the process by providing leadership and setting a system of financial incentives to the states that encouraged reforms. NEM was established in 1998, trade across the NEM area was liberalised and uniform regulations were set for generation and transmission activities. Interstate transmission gets the same treatment as any other transmission assets, and there are no interstate tariffs. As discussed above, transmission links between the states are still weak limiting trade between the states in peak demand periods. But some new transmission capacity is currently being built and more is planned.

In the US, the Federal Energy Regulatory Commission (FERC) has played a key role in promoting the integration of electricity markets. In 1996, FERC issued wholesale open-access rules requiring transmission owners to provide point-to-point and network services under the same conditions they provide for themselves, and to separate their transmission and supply activities. To avoid discrimination in network access, FERC encouraged, but did not mandate, the creation of Independent System Operators (ISO). In December 1999, FERC issued Order 2000 on Regional Transmission Organisations (RTO). These measures have contributed to an increase in electricity trade across the US, particularly in the western and north-eastern states, and has greatly increased the need for transmission links between the various electricity systems. Federal legislation is being considered to reinforce interstate electricity trade such as the proposed Electric Power Market Competition and Reliability Act.

Experience in OECD countries shows that political willingness is a key to successfully developing regional markets. Success can be achieved through informal co-operation but political agreement is necessary to develop common approaches on pricing and access to cross-border lines and the basic rules governing each of the national or state markets. The task of establishing a regional electricity market is simpler within federal countries, where the federal government can provide financial incentives, propose federal legislation to speed up the process and serve as a focal point for co-ordination.

■ Regulation of Cross-border Links

Conditions for access to cross-border transmission links and the pricing of interconnection must be set to achieve efficient operation of regional markets. These conditions are a key determinant of the incentives to invest in interconnectors.

International and interstate links raise similar issues and so this section considers both. There is, however, one important difference in that, while interstate links can be subject to the same (federal) regulations, the operation of international links generally depends on international agreements.

Effective market integration requires open access to interconnectors. In addition, transmission capacity needs to be allocated flexibly to the most valuable use at each point in time. This is consistent with the use of nodal prices and auctions to allocate capacity but conflicts with long-term physical capacity allocations that give priority to some users at the expense of others. Ideally, prices should depend only on costs and be independent of whether trade takes place locally or involves various countries or states. Otherwise, trade would be discouraged by the "pancaking" of transmission rates (adding the charges of various transmission companies to the price of a single energy transfer). Pricing principles for interconnectors and the shared network should be the same in an integrated market.

Interconnectors can be regulated or commercial. The recovery of investments made in regulated interconnectors is secured by regulation. For commercial interconnectors, it depends on commercial transactions.

Regulated interconnectors can be treated as part of the shared network, so that there are no cross-border tariffs, or can be treated separately. The first approach applies, for instance, to the links among the Nordic countries and to most of the links among the Australian states that belong to NEM. This is also the basic approach being considered in the EU. The second approach, which results in "pancaked" tariffs, is applied in the California market and the mid-Atlantic states of the US, among others.

Commercial interconnectors generally operate on the basis of long-term contracts and international agreements. These give priority access to some specified parties and indicate how prices (or compensation in kind) are to be determined. Unused capacity can be sold to other parties through an auction or other means. This is the approach for the interconnectors between France and Spain, between the Nordic countries and other neighbouring countries, between England & Wales and Scotland and between England & Wales and France. Commercial arrangements for interconnectors are sometimes challenged before the courts on the grounds that they impose limitations on third-party access. Commercial arrangements may also be modified by regulatory decisions. For instance, arrangements for interconnectors within the EU could be modified by the development of common rules. But the scope of such changes depends on the nature of pre-existing legal rights.

Commercial interconnectors can also operate on a merchant basis. This is a new approach that is now being tested in Australia. It aims to promote transmission investment while minimising regulatory involvement. Only one line, connecting Queensland and New South Wales, has been built on this basis, but more are under consideration. A merchant interconnector gets its revenue from buying energy at one end of the line and selling it at the other. Profits are made only if there are price differences between the two ends of the line.

There are fundamental differences among the various approaches. Regulated interconnectors integrated into the network and merchant interconnectors provide open access and, therefore, an adequate basis for organising transactions in a regional market. Commercial interconnectors linked to long-term access contracts are not, in practice, providers of open access and can be a barrier to the development of regional markets. However, when markets are not equally open at both ends of the link, these arrangements may be more appropriate.

Incentives to invest are presumably higher when the investment is protected by regulation or by a long-term contract than when it depends on spot market rates. Despite the obvious advantages of merchant interconnectors, the higher investment risk may slow down their development.

■ Reliability

Regionalisation and competition change the way in which electricity systems are operated and investment decisions are made. The institutions that manage and monitor the reliability of electricity systems have to adapt to these changes. Increased regional trade makes system operators more dependent on conditions outside their control area. System operation has to be adapted to increasing energy flows into and out of the system. Long-term reliability and investment needs become increasingly dependent on generation capacity situated outside the system and on the transmission capacity available to export and import energy. As a result, increased regional co-operation among system operators is needed. This can be achieved through extensive and intensive communication among the various system operators, as in the Nordic countries, or through the merger of the operators into a single entity, as in the Australian National Electricity Market.

Competition also has an impact on the way that the institutions responsible for reliability interact. In the past, reliability issues were addressed through co-operation among vertically integrated electricity companies. In a regional market, these companies become competitors, and this reduces their incentives to co-operate voluntarily. Co-operation becomes more difficult as it may conflict with competition law.

Competition also creates a need for transparency and neutrality. This obligation affects the way system operators and organisations conduct their business. Decisions have to be based on objective criteria known to all parties and this limits the scope for informal co-operation.

Intersystem reliability has to be managed differently after competition develops. The separation of system operators and transmission companies from generation provides an adequate basis for dealing with these issues. There are no legal impediments to co-operation among independent system operators and transmission companies, and their incentives to co-operate are largely unaffected by market competition.

The institutions dealing with reliability may themselves need to be reformed. In the US, there are plans to reform the North American Reliability Council (NERC). The aim is transform it from an industry co-operative body to an independent organisation subject only to regulatory oversight. Some changes have also taken place in Europe. The members of the Union for the Co-ordination of the Transmission of Electricity (UCTE), the intersystem reliability organisation covering most of Continental OECD Europe (except the Nordic countries), now includes only transmission companies and system operators. The European Transmission System Operators Association (ETSO) was created in 1999, including the whole of OECD Europe and some additional Eastern European countries. In the future, as the integration of the EU electricity market moves forward, intersystem reliability issues will become more important.

Long-term Issues in Transmission Investment: Planning, Development and Ownership

There are three broad approaches to the organisation of transmission and transmission investment depending on the degree of disaggregation or unbundling in each country. The leading role in planning and developing transmission expansion can be taken by a vertically-integrated transmission company, or a transmission company that owns and operates the network, or can shared between a system operator with some planning responsibility and a number of transmission owners.

Transmission and generation are vertically integrated in the first approach and separate in the second. Integration in the Independent System Operator or ISO approach lies somewhere in between full integration and no integration at all. In the ISO approach, generators are the owners of transmission assets but the right to decide on the use of transmission assets is largely transferred to the ISO and, therefore, the owners rights are limited. Table 1 summarises the organisation of transmission ownership and investment in some electricity systems.

Figure 11

Ownership and Operation of Transmission in the EU

* *Vertically integrated means that transmission owners also own generation assets and control system operation, regardless of whether there is legal, accounting or other form of separation.*

Source: IEA.

■ Model 1: Vertically Integrated Company

In one group of electricity systems, companies are vertically integrated and perform all transmission-related activities, often through a separate company subsidiary. These companies own and operate transmission infrastructure and are responsible for planning and developing the system, generally subject to approval by the relevant authority or in collaboration with it. This is the approach taken in Japan, Canada (excepting Ontario) and several European countries – Austria, Belgium, Denmark, France, Germany, Hungary, Ireland, Greece, Ireland, Portugal and Switzerland –.

Separate accounting of transmission activities is the minimum requirement in most of these countries[34]. This means keeping separate accounts for generation and transmission activities within the same vertically-integrated entity. On this basis, electricity companies charge themselves the same prices for transmission as they do to others and offer separate prices for generation and transmission services. In practice, many electricity systems have chosen to establish a separate transmission company subsidiary to carry out transmission activities. This separates employees involved in transmission from those involved in other activities.

In France, for example, the network is managed by the Gestionnaire du Réseau de Transport (GRT), who is also responsible for its development. GRT is owned by Electricité de France (EDF). The director of GRT is nominated by EDF and appointed by the energy minister, after consultation with the regulator. The general lines of transmission development have to be approved by the ministry and, within this framework, annual investment plans are approved by the regulator. In some countries, such as Germany, investment plans are laid out by electricity companies and do not require government approval.

34. *With the exception of Japan.*

■ Model 2: Transmission Company

In another group of systems, a separate transmission company, with no interest in generation or other ESI activities, owns transmission assets and operates the system. These transmission companies are generally responsible for planning and developing transmission subject to approval by the relevant authority. The aim of this approach is to separate transmission from potentially competitive activities, namely generation. Variations of this model have been adopted in several Australian states, in England & Wales, Finland, the Netherlands, New Zealand, Norway, Ontario, Spain, and Sweden.

In England & Wales the National Grid Company (NGC) is the owner of the transmission system, operates it and is responsible for both the planning and the development of the network. The regulator (Ofgem) sets a maximum allowance for capital expenditure in transmission intended to limit investment costs and to provide incentives for cost efficiency. Norway and Spain also apply incentive regulation (a revenue cap). In other countries, such as Australia, Finland and Sweden, revenues are determined within a cost-of-service framework.

Variations of this approach can be found in the Australian state of Victoria, Spain and New Zealand. In Spain and Victoria, development of the network can be auctioned and conducted by a different company. In addition, the transmission company in Victoria is not responsible for planning. Planning is the responsibility of a separate organisation (VENcorp). In New Zealand, planning is conducted by the transmission company, but it can proceed only if end users commit themselves to pay for the investments.

■ Model 3: Independent System Operator

Some US markets (Nepool and PJM) and Italy have chosen to separate ownership from operation of the transmission system. The aim of operational separation is to allow for a dispersed ownership of transmission assets and a decentralised development of the network, without forcing generators to divest their transmission assets. It opens investment to third parties, pays market prices to transmission owners and places the assets under the control of an ISO. Planning or at least planning approval is the responsibility of the not-for-profit system operator and the network is developed by the owners. This approach allows generation and transmission assets to be vertically integrated but requires system operation to be separated from transmission ownership. The "transmission company" approach, by contrast, does not allow joint ownership of generation and transmission but allows system operation to be managed by transmission owners.

As an example, the Independent System Operator (ISO) in PJM operates the transmission assets of seven different owners and is responsible for planning the grid. Transmission owners are obliged to execute these plans. There is a two-tier approach to governance. An independent board, which has ultimate decision-making authority, co-exists with a committee of stakeholders, which makes decisions. The board does not review every decision of the committee.

In Italy, most transmission assets are owned by the national electricity company, ENEL, now being privatised. A public company, the Gestore della Rete Nazionale, is the system operator and makes development decisions, which are executed by transmission owners.

Figure 12

Models of Transmission Organisation

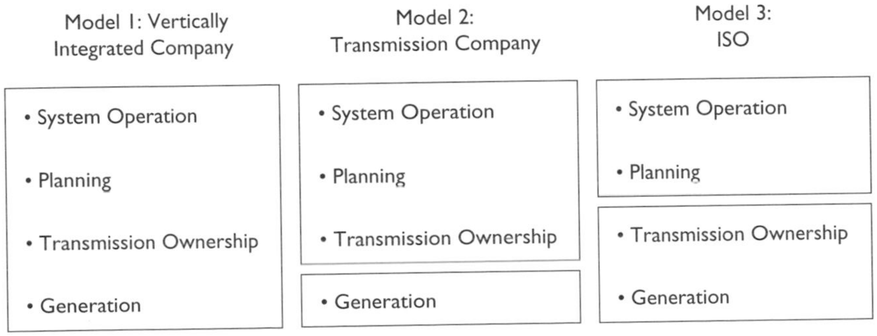

Model 1: Vertically Integrated Company	Model 2: Transmission Company	Model 3: ISO
• System Operation • Planning • Transmission Ownership • Generation	• System Operation • Planning • Transmission Ownership	• System Operation • Planning
	• Generation	• Transmission Ownership • Generation

Source: IEA.

Table 7

Examples of the Organisation of Transmission in IEA Countries

	Approach: Investment led by	Transmission owner(s)	Transmission planner	Transmission authorisation	Transmission developer
Victoria (Australia)	Transmission Company	GPU Powernet	VENCorp	VENCorp	Competitive, building by independent companies
Denmark	Transmission owners	Elkraft, Eltra and regional transmission companies	System operators (Elkraft and Eltra)	Danish Energy Agency	Transmission owners
Finland	Transmission company	Fingrid	Fingrid	Fingrid	Generally Fingrid
France	Vertically-integrated company	Electricité de France (EDF)	Gestionnaire du Réseau de Transport (GRT), within EDF	Energy minister and regulator	Gestionnaire du Réseau de Transport (GRT), within EDF
Italy	System operator	ENEL and others	ISO (Gestore della Rete Nazionale)	ISO (Gestore della Rete Nazionale)	Transmission owners
Japan	Vertically-integrated companies	Nine electricity companies	Electricity companies	Energy ministry (METI)	Electricity companies
New Zealand	Transmission company	Transpower	Users	Users	Competitive, building by independent companies

Table 7

Examples of the Organisation of Transmission in IEA Countries

	Approach: Investment led by	Transmission owner(s)	Transmission planner	Transmission authorisation	Transmission developer
Norway	Transmission Company (Statnett)	Statnett	Statnett	Energy ministry (NVE)	Generally Statnett
Spain	Transmission company (Red Electrica)	Red Electrica and Others	Red Electrica	Ministry of Economics	Competitive, building by independent companies
Sweden	Transmission company (Svenska Kraftnät)	Svenska Kraftnät	Svenska Kraftnät	Svenska Kraftnät	Svenska Kraftnät
UK, England & Wales	Transmission Company (National Grid Company, NGC)	NGC	NGC	NGC subject to regulator setting a capital expenditure allowance	NGC
US, PJM	Independent System operator (ISO-PJM)	Seven transmission owners	ISO-PJM	ISO-PJM	Transmission owners

Source: A. Henney (2000), EU Commission (2000) and IEA.

■ Role of Markets in Transmission Investment

In all electricity systems, responsibility for transmission planning and reliability is allocated to a single party, usually the system operator, who may also be the owner of transmission and generation assets. The process of transmission investment differs from the decentralised and market-driven dynamics of investment in many other industries. It reflects the special characteristics of the transmission network and, particularly, the monopolistic nature of system operation.

Within this framework, a number of recent reforms have been initiated to increase the reliance of transmission on markets. The ISO approach, in particular, aims to open investment in transmission to a larger number of potential investors. Investment in transmission assets can be driven, at least in principle, by markets. But to make this approach work, a number of "market imperfections" that may have a detrimental impact on transmission investment have to be dealt with. One key issue is that incentives to invest may be reduced if some industry players enjoy excessive market power. Players with market power may have incentives to under-invest and to artificially create congestion by reducing the availability of transmission and generation capacity in potentially congested locations. Congestion brings higher transmission prices and/or higher energy prices. So, transmission owners and generators may profit from congestion rents if they do not behave competitively.

Excessive market power is a potentially significant issue for transmission investment in many electricity markets around the world in which the ownership of generation and transmission assets is relatively concentrated and the "contestability" of markets by new entrants is limited. Market power can be effectively addressed by promoting a more dispersed ownership of transmission and generation assets and providing a framework that facilitates timely entry of new players into the electricity supply industry.

Assessment

In a world without trade and competition in electricity, a vertically-integrated industry would solve many of the issues related to transmission investment. Vertical integration unifies the roles of planner, owner, system operator and developer within a single decision-maker, allowing for the "internalisation" of network and generation decisions in a simple and straightforward way. In addition, vertically-integrated companies normally have strong incentives to invest and sustain reliability. This is the scheme that has dominated the industry worldwide until the 1990s.

A vertically integrated ESI complicates the development of trade and competition. Fair and non-discriminatory access to the network is essential for the development of free electricity markets. However, transmission remains a monopoly, even in a liberalised ESI. If the transmission monopoly is vertically integrated with the competitive activities of generation, it has an incentive to use its monopoly power against competitors. A network monopolist can distort competition in many ways. Discriminatory access conditions, high or discriminatory access charges and "strategic" investment in grid augmentation may put competitors at a disadvantage.

The issue is how to ensure non-discriminatory network access while, at the same time, sustaining incentives for the efficient development of the network. Each of the three models strikes a different balance between these goals.

In the vertically-integrated approach to transmission, incentives to invest are not generally an issue, but the owner of transmission may be tempted to discriminate against competitors. So, the vertically integrated approach is usually supplemented with measures to foster trade and competition. The separation of the accounting and management of transmission reduces, to some extent, the transmission owner's ability to discriminate. The application ex post of competition law may deter discriminatory behaviour. This, however, requires significant involvement of regulatory and competition authorities and, in the end, may fail to prevent discrimination. The transmission company and ISO models eliminate the incentive of the transmission services provider to discriminate. This is achieved by unbundling either the whole transmission function or by separating the operation of the network from other commercial interests. Unbundling eliminates concerns about discrimination but creates a need for co-ordination between the unbundled functions.

The "transmission company" approach offers a workable compromise between the various policy goals. On the one hand, generation is unbundled to promote competitive neutrality in the provision of transmission services. On the other hand, most network-related activities – planning, investment, operation and maintenance – are conducted within an integrated framework. This facilitates proper management of the tradeoffs between the costs of network expansion and the costs of system operation. Under this approach the complexity of the decision-making process and the institutional framework is limited compared to those of the ISO approach.

In practice, establishing a transmission company may be difficult in countries like the US where the ownership of transmission assets is initially dispersed among several private parties. In this case, establishing a transmission company requires that existing owners agree to sell the assets at a reasonable price. By contrast, when the ESI is publicly owned, establishing a transmission company only requires a government policy decision.

The ISO approach allows joint ownership of generation and transmission. It also creates a market for investment in which the planner (the ISO) may play only a residual role. Market prices can provide signals to investors on where and when investment is needed. Market prices are higher at congested nodes of the grid: this encourages users of the network to develop cheaper alternatives, notably additional transmission and/or generating capacity. This may have some advantages over centralised planning of network development.

The ISO approach requires a complex set of institutions and market mechanisms. Developing an effective ISO governance structure requires striking a delicate balance among three overlapping goals: ensuring neutrality, protecting the interest of stakeholders, including transmission owners, and providing incentives for efficient ISO management. Neutrality is important because it is the basis for non-discriminatory access. Protecting stakeholders is important because the ISO makes decisions with large financial implications but has no matching financial responsibilities. Providing incentives to management is important because ISOs are not-for-profit and there is no clear owner. Governance structures for ISOs are still being developed and tested so that there is still some uncertainty on which approaches are most effective.

Under the ISO approach, the centralised operation of the network may reduce the incentives of third parties to invest in transmission. The ISO, rather than the owner, has control over the use of transmission assets. Thus, ownership does not guarantee access to transmission. A generator who owns a transmission line connecting him to a consumer may, nonetheless, not be able to deliver his power, due to system constraints. Decisions taken by the system operator concerning the use of a line are not necessarily those that would be taken by its owners. Anticipation that these problems may occur could discourage investment. This issue and, more generally, the problems created by the unfeasibility of firmly guaranteeying transmission rights to market players, can be addressed by the sophisticated pricing of transmission rights[35].

The organisation of transmission investment is being adapted to accommodate trade and competition. There is no perfect solution, but a number of workable solutions are being developed. Experience with vertically integrated electricity companies and

35. These complex issues have been widely discussed in the literature on transmission rights. See for instance Chao, Peck, Oren and Wilson:"Flow based transmission rights and congestion management" (The Electricity Journal, October 2000) and the references therein.

with transmission companies suggests that investment performance should not be an issue, provided that adequate regulatory monitoring and incentives continue to be provided. The development of the ISO approach and some experiments being conducted within the transmission-company framework indicate that transmission investment can be driven, to a much larger extent than was previously recognised, by markets. These are, however, new and still largely untested structures that need to be monitored and progressively adjusted to ensure proper performance.

CASE STUDIES

This chapter presents a detailed analysis of the performance of six competitive electricity markets. First, the case of England & Wales illustrates how markets can sustain investment and reliability over a long period provided prices are high enough to reward investors and the regulatory and policy frameworks allow investment to flow into the market. The British experience also shows that a relatively high degree of regulatory intervention can be compatible with strong private investment activity, provided the general direction of policy is clear and that the authorisations and regulatory processes are not too lengthy.

The cases of Sweden and Norway provide an interesting example of the development of a common regulatory framework and the integration of markets. The Nordic case is characterised by low investment activity, in a context of low prices, strong reserves at the onset of competition and regionalisation. Investment has been weak and largely driven by government policies and subsidies. The Nordic market also illustrates the challenges involved in setting up ambitious policies to influence the choice of fuels in a market context.

The other three cases examined rely on a much shorter record. Some of the most interesting issues are still only developing and no firm assessment is possible.

The Australian experience demonstrates the interplay between prices and investment activity, in a complex setting in which different states present different supply and demand balances. In addition, the Australian case exposes the difficulties in integrating previously isolated markets but also shows that the issues can be coped with.

Two sharply contrasting American markets are discussed. California provides some important illustrations of the problems that may emerge during reform. Complex and slow authorisation processes played a major role in the capacity shortage that took place in 2000 and early 2001. PJM, on the other hand, has performed smoothly in a context of sustainable prices, minimal policy barriers to entry and a fairly speedy authorisation process. In contrast to regulatory risk in California, which is generally perceived as high, regulatory risk in PJM is seen as low because the reforms that were implemented there minimised changes to the institutional and company structure.

The United Kingdom: England & Wales

■ Structure of the Industry

Industry Restructuring Since the Late 1980s

The UK encompasses three different geographical systems of generation, transmission and supply of electricity: England & Wales, Scotland, and Northern Ireland. The focus here is on the England & Wales system that was restructured and privatised as of March 1990. The national monopoly until then, the Central Electricity Generating Board (CEGB), was split into four companies: National Power and PowerGen, Nuclear Electric which was granted all nuclear generation, and the National Grid Company (NGC) which owns and operates the transmission network. Twelve Regional Electricity Companies replaced the Area Electricity Boards, which had been responsible for electricity distribution. Ordinary shares in the National Grid were transferred to the Regional Electricity Companies (RECs). During 1990, an electricity spot market, known as the Pool, was also established. The Pool was a mandatory auction market with limited demand-side participation and in which prices included a capacity payment to generators.

In parallel to the introduction of competition in generation, the retail market was gradually opened to competition. From April 1990, customers with peak loads of more than 1 MW (about 45 per cent of the non-domestic market) were able to choose their supplier. In 1999-2000, the Office of Gas and Electricity Markets (OFGEM) estimated that 80 per cent of these customers had switched to a company other than their local REC. The threshold was lowered in April 1994 to customers with peak loads of more than 100 kW, of which 67 per cent had switched by 1999/2000. Between September 1998 and May 1999, the rest of the electricity market was opened to competition.

In March 2001, the introduction in England & Wales of the New Electricity Trading Arrangements (NETA) altered the organisation of trade in the electricity industry. The new arrangements are based on bilateral trading between generators, suppliers, traders and customers.

Current Industry Structure

As the figures below illustrate, the industry changed radically following restructuring. At the time of privatisation, the market was highly concentrated, with the two largest generating companies supplying nearly three-quarters of the market. Since then, a number of new producers have entered the market, together with a large number of 'autogenerators' which produce electricity mainly for their own use. The number of major power producers – companies whose main business is generation – has increased from six before privatisation to 11 in 1991, 20 in 1993 and 30 in mid-2000[36].

In England & Wales, the three largest generators in 2000 were National Power, PowerGen, and British Energy, accounting altogether for slightly less than 50 per cent of the market. In 2000, new entrants generated nearly 15 per cent of market output. In addition, Électricité de France (EDF), together with the generation businesses of Scottish Power (SP) and Scottish and Southern Energy (SSE) have a number of contracts to sell electricity through the interconnectors to suppliers in England & Wales.

36. *UK Energy Report (2000).*

Figure 13

Shares of Generation Output in England and Wales

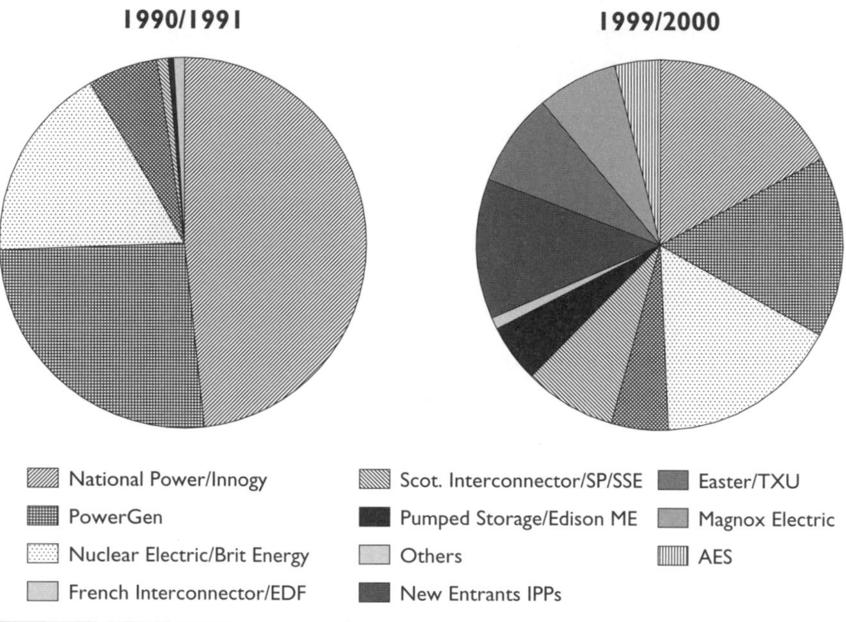

Source: Data from the Pool's statistical digests.

National Grid, the independent transmission company, is also responsible for system operation. There is regulated third-party access to the network. Distribution is unbundled and there are rules to limit "self dealing"[37] by distribution companies.

Institutional Structure

In England & Wales, the regulation of industry is conducted primarily through the licensing of generation, transmission and supply. Entry into generation is subject to an authorisation procedure that may take into account energy specific criteria such as which fuel is to be used. At the time of reform, a new actor was created by the

37. *That is, purchasing energy from their own generation units.*

Electricity Act, the Director General of Electricity Supply (DGES), heading the Office of Electricity Regulation. This office merged with the gas regulator in 1999 to form OFGEM. As a result, there are three main institutional players in the market, the Department of Trade and Industry (DTI), the independent regulator, and the Competition Commission, which replaced the Monopolies and Mergers Commission (MMC) in 1999.

DTI is the responsible ministry with overall supervisory and executive functions on energy policy. It has a leading role in the ongoing review of energy regulation and in pressing forward with the legislative reform of energy regulation. In addition, the consent or agreement of DTI's secretary of state is required for key regulatory decisions, such as the licensing of generators, transmission and electricity supply companies. Alternatively the Ministry may issue licences with the consent of the DGES. OFGEM is in charge of promoting competition in all parts of the gas and electricity industries by creating the conditions for companies to compete fairly and for customers to make an informed choice among suppliers. It is also responsible for regulating industry segments where competition is not effective by setting price controls and standards to protect customers and ensure reliability.

OFGEM is mainly concerned with economic regulation, which is conducted primarily through licence conditions and regulations on prices, access, service quality and other economic variables. The DGES also has powers, concurrent with the Director General of Fair Trading (DGFT), to apply and enforce the Competition Act. The DGFT alone, however, has powers to issue guidance on penalties and to make and amend its own procedural rules. The DGES has, on at least one occasion, formally and publicly threatened licensees to make a "monopoly reference" before the Competition Commission to force generators to make divestitures. It has also imposed other structural measures, such as limits imposed on ownership of generation by electricity suppliers, and enforced similar limits contained in the original licences.

More recently, OFGEM has been pushing the introduction of a market abuse licence condition for certain electricity generator licences. This proposal for a 'good behaviour' clause that would commit generators to act "competitively" in all circumstances has been very controversial. It was eventually rejected in an appeal to the Competition Commission on substantive grounds. However, following governmental support by the Secretary of Trade in 2001, it is now expected to be introduced by OFGEM and the government in a manner that will not require a reference to the Competition Commission.

■ Entry and Investment

Investment and System Development Process

There is no formal planning of system development or monitoring of investment plans. The initiative for proposals for new generation capacity is left entirely to the developers[38]. NGC, the grid owner and system operator, issues annual statements of needs for the next seven years as well as forecasts of likely developments in generation and plans for future investment in transmission. The company is formally responsible for adequacy of transmission services, that is, it must ensure that transmission capacity is adequate to meet electricity demand. Until 2001, formal responsibility for generation adequacy was with the RECs; they were deemed to meet it as long as they bought from the Pool and the price was less than the Value of Lost Load.

NGC's estimates of future capacity additions are uncertain for several reasons. First, notification of a proposal does not always translate into the actual construction of capacity. In addition, the timing of projects is always uncertain. Lastly, the estimates do not take account the possibility of modifications of connection agreements and possible future closures, for which only six months' notice is required. On this basis, OFGEM

38. *See DTI (1998).*

considers that NGC's estimates are likely to overstate new entry, whilst acknowledging that predicting entry is difficult since conditions inviting or deterring it could change rapidly–notably movements in gas prices.

The construction of an electricity generating plant in the UK is subject to a two-fold authorisation before construction can commence. On the one hand, promoters of generation projects need to obtain consent. Consent is given by the Secretary of State for Trade and Industry for plants above 50 MW. For smaller projects, the local planning authorities are in charge. In both cases an environmental impact assessment is required. When consent is issued, it lasts for five years; within this time a project must show signs of actual construction[39].

Under the Energy Act 1976, the project must also be notified to the Secretary of State for 'clearance'. According to OFGEM, the time taken to obtain the approvals to build a new plant ranges from three to six months where there is no objections or specific concerns about a project, but could be significantly longer[40].

Electricity generators are subject to a licensing regime. Licences can be granted by either the Secretary of State or by the regulator under general authority from the Secretary of State. They set out the obligations and duties of the licensed generator. Most licences issued are of a standard form, with the notable exception of those issued at the time of privatization[41]. Since implementation of the Utilities Act in April 2001, licences take the form of references to a set of Standard Conditions determined by the Secretary of State, plus any special conditions particular to that licence[42].

---

39. *Competition Commission (2001).*

40. *See Competition Commission (2001).*

41. *There are 15 non standard generation licences presently in existence: British Energy Generation (UK) Ltd; British Energy Generation Ltd; Deeside Power Development Company Ltd; Diamond Power Generation; Emerald Power Generation; Jade Power Generation; First Hydro; Magnox Electric plc; National Power plc; PowerGen UK plc; Fife Power; Grangemouth CHP; London Underground; Midlands Power (UK); and Seeboard Powerlink.*

42. *This follows the present gas licensing model. Another major change introduced by the Utilities Act 2000 is that the activity of distribution is now a separately licensable activity.*

Main Constraints on Investment

Since the 1980s, different regulatory and policy constraints have been imposed on the electricity market which might have altered investment decisions. These include coal contracts, temporary price caps, so-called Non Fossil Fuel Obligations or NFFOs, and the temporary gas moratorium discussed below.

Contracts to ensure coal use in power generation were imposed at the time of privatisation, in order to support the domestic coal industry. This constraint had a negative effect on investment in gas fired plants; however, it was gradually relaxed.

No price control on generation was put in place by government at the time of restructuring. Price caps were agreed in the Pool, however, over the period 1994-1996. The government suspected wholesale price rises in 1993 were due to the exercise of market power by generators. The price caps were set at 2.4 pence/kWh (time-weighted) and 2.55 pence/kWh (demand-weighted). After price regulation was removed, generators continued to comply with these caps.

Following its Review of Energy Sources for Power Generation, the government adopted a stricter policy on licensing of new gas-fired generation from October 1998 to the introduction of NETA in March 2001. The report raised concerns that the contribution of coal to diversity of supply and energy security was under threat following the dramatic change in power generation mix since reform. The operation of the Pool was perceived by government to be the main cause of distortion, as it kept wholesale prices high, and this in turn encouraged the construction of new gas-fired capacity at the expense of existing coal-fired plants. The new policy, which was intended to be temporary, was meant to sustain coal generation while the electricity market was being reformed[43]. Restrictions did not apply to combined

43. The programme announced by the White Paper comprised: (i) the reform of the electricity trading arrangements in England and Wales; (ii) seeking practical opportunities for divestment by the major coal-fired generators; (iii) pressing ahead with competition in electricity supply for all customers; (iv) separating supply and distribution in electricity markets (as now achieved through the Utilities Act described above); (v) resolving technical system stability issues around the growth of gas generation, including the proper remuneration of flexible plant; and (vi) continuing to press for an open heat and power (CHP) projects, dual-firing stations, and certain gas-fired black start projects, as they supported environmental or security of supply objectives.

In 1990, government set a target of 1,000 MW of renewables capacity in 2000. The non-fossil fuel obligation (NFFO) was extended to include renewables as well as nuclear energy, funded by the fossil fuel levy. It empowers the government to require public electricity suppliers to obtain specified amounts of renewable generation capacity from specified non-fossil sources, a guaranteed price being paid to non-fossil generators. Most funds went to nuclear until its privatisation. Since then, a large share of funds went to renewables.

The NFFO was replaced by the Utilities Act 2000, which allows the Secretary of State to impose on suppliers an obligation that a specified proportion of the electricity they supply must be generated from renewable sources. This obligation will be imposed gradually to meet the government's goal of having 5 per cent of the UK's electricity needs met by renewable power in 2003. The goal is to reach 10% by 2010. It will be supported by a system of tradable 'green certificates'.

Market Design

The electricity spot market in England & Wales – the Pool – was a compulsory trading mechanism for generators and suppliers, regulated by its members and operated by NGC. The Pool set prices for energy for each half-hour period on the basis of a daily day-ahead auction. Generators submitted bids specifying the capacity available for the next day and the price at which they were willing to sell output from each capacity unit. Bids were fixed for the day; in other words, the same prices applied to all half-hour periods[44].

energy market in Europe. Since then, NETA were implemented. In addition, important developments occurred in relation to the divestment of plant by the major coal-fired generators (a total of 10.65 GW of plant being divested in the financial year 1999/00), competition in electricity supply (statistics showing that by the end of March 2000, 5.2 million customers switched supplier), separation of supply and distribution, and in pressing for an open market in Europe.

44. The unconstrained merit order may not be feasible due to network capacity constraints (ignored by the pool). If needed, the grid operator calculates a constrained merit order. "Constrained on" units are paid their bid price plus the capacity payment and "constrained off" units receive the pool purchasing price minus their bid.

With some limited exceptions, there was no demand-side bidding. Bid prices contained several terms such as a fixed start-up rate, a no-load rate for each hour that the unit was running at its technical minimum and various energy rates for different loads. The Pool combined the bids to construct an unconstrained merit order of generating plants that minimised the cost of serving the scheduled demand for each period.

Price bids were firm, yet capacity bids could be withdrawn up to the moment of operation. Buyers of electricity paid the Pool Selling Price (PSP), defined as the Pool Purchasing price plus Uplift. Uplift was the cost of the various services provided by the system operator, constraints costs and transmission losses. Scheduled generators received the Pool Purchasing Price (PPP), defined as the System Marginal Price (SMP) – the price of the highest bid needed to cover scheduled demand, where prices for start up and no load are averaged and added to energy prices – plus an administered capacity payment. The Pool was replaced by NETA in March 2001, on the alleged grounds that it discriminated against coal-fired generation and that electricity prices were too high as a direct result of the way it operated.

The capacity payment was provided to all power stations which were available, whether or not they actually generated electricity. Capacity payments were defined by a complex set of rules ultimately aimed at reflecting the expected cost to the user of a supply interruption. This value was calculated as the product of two quantities: the value of loss load (VOLL), measured in pounds sterling per kWh, and the loss of load probability (LOLP). VOLL was set administratively, as there was no demand-side bidding from which the actual figure could be inferred. This value was set at £2,000/MWh in 1990 and was then increased annually by the RPI – in 2000, it stood at £2,816/MWh.

LOLP was meant to take into account how much capacity was available relative to forecast demand and was hence higher when capacity was scarce. This amount (LOLP x VOLL) was charged on all energy sold and paid to the owners of all capacity that had been declared available but had not been scheduled. The size of capacity payments varied greatly, depending on available capacity relative to demand as measured through LOLP.

The capacity mechanism was widely criticised for not providing the right incentives to investors, notably because it was prone to manipulation. It was subsequently abandoned when the Pool was replaced by NETA. Anomalous results had occurred, due in part to the complex rules governing the calculation of the likelihood of particular stations being available. The LOLP reflected the probability for each half-hour that there would be insufficient generation to meet demand, on the basis on NGC's demand forecasts and generator's bids. The value of LOLP was affected not only by the reserve margin but also by the mix of plant, each plant being assigned a measure of its reliability known as the disappearance ratio.

Capacity payments were highly sensitive to the withdrawal of particular generating plants and often did not reflect underlying market conditions. They were prone to manipulation through capacity withholding. Stations that were commissioned before April 1992 had fixed disappearance ratios, whilst the others had 'live' disappearance ratios that could vary according to their operating performance. As occurred in summer 1999, an unplanned outage at a relatively new plant in one month could significantly increase capacity payments in the following month, despite high reliability of the plant on a day-to-day basis. Furthermore, when an older plant was replaced by a newer one, capacity payments increased despite there being no change in the capacity available.

Wholesale electricity prices and the abuse of market power were subjects of great concern. Pool prices started at a low level in 1990, but they rose steadily and remained high during the whole period. This led to investigations by MMC and the regulator. It could be argued that electricity pricing in the Pool was distorted by oligopolistic behaviour, particularly in the first years of the Pool when market concentration was high. The resulting high prices could explain why investment has been relatively steady.

Until NETA, price risks were managed in a financial market that ran in parallel to the Pool. Bilateral contracts were used by generators and buyers of electricity the opportunity to hedge the risk of price fluctuations. From 80 to 90 per cent of electricity trades were hedged with contracts for differences (CfDs), which allowed participants to trade at prices less volatile than the Pool's half-hourly prices[45]. Indeed, the parties to a two-way CfD would agree on a strike price for a fixed quantity of electricity. Whenever the Pool price fell below the strike price the buyer paid the seller the difference between the two. Whenever the Pool price was higher the seller refunded the difference. Hence, a generator's revenues would be fixed by the strike price if he produced the required amount of electricity, while the Pool price still determined the generator's incentives at the margin.

The new system, adopted in March 2001, can be managed on the basis of bilateral trade in addition to forwards and futures markets. Risk can now be managed through bilateral contracts between generators and suppliers or large customers for the physical delivery of electricity. Power producers can also practice near real-time trading – up to 3¹/₂ hours before real time – on the forward market. In addition, NGC manages a balancing mechanism operating 3¹/₂ hours ahead of real time and up to real time, to ensure the security of the system. Derivatives markets are expected to develop to enable market participants to manage commercial risks. The new arrangements leave the issue of adequate supply entirely up to market forces. Capacity payments have been abandoned and so there is no guaranteed revenue for availability.

The numerous investigations into the Pool's operations, threats to refer the companies to the competition authorities and the changes in trading arrangements have certainly created some regulatory risk and may have affected investment decisions.

---

45. Green (1999).

■ Performance

In the last fifteen years, demand for electricity has grown slowly and regularly at rates averaging 2.3 per cent. Capacity additions, while showing more variation over time, have been large both before and after vesting.

Capacity utilisation, defined as the ratio between annual energy production and total generation capacity multiplied by the total time it could be used, is an indicator of efficiency. Greater use of capacity implies greater productive efficiency. In the UK, capacity utilisation has fluctuated in the last fifteen years. It was declining before 1989. After privatisation, capacity utilisation rose above 50 per cent. In the last two years, however, it declined to around 50 per cent.

Reserve margins are a key indicator of whether there are sufficient reserves to cover peak demand. In the UK, reserve margins have fluctuated over the last fifteen years, yet remained high. After restructuring, reserve margins slightly decreased, nearing 20 per cent in the mid-1990s but increased again in recent years, to around 25 per cent in 2000. Fluctuations within this range reflect changes in demand as well as variations in capacity and do not seem to follow any definite pattern. The same sort of random fluctuations in reserve levels were observed before competition.

The evidence to date is that potential developers of new generation in England & Wales have been able to secure sites and the necessary consents. Any generator who meets the technical requirements to connect has been able to do so, subject to there being sufficient transmission capacity available[46]. In addition, securing project financing did not appear to be a problem.

In the UK, growth in generation capacity has mainly taken the form of investment in gas-fired plants. Change in the generation mix has been significant, with the progressive replacement of coal-fired plants by gas-fired ones and, to a lesser extent by switching from oil to gas.

46. *Competition Commission (2000).*

Figure 14

Demand and Generation Capacity in the UK, 1985-2000

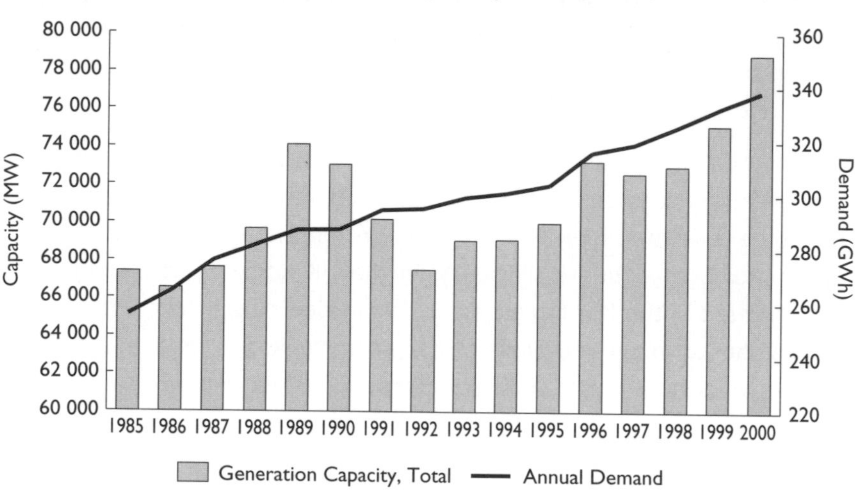

Source: Data from Department of Trade and Industry (2001).

Figure 15

Capacity Utilisation in the UK, 1985-2000

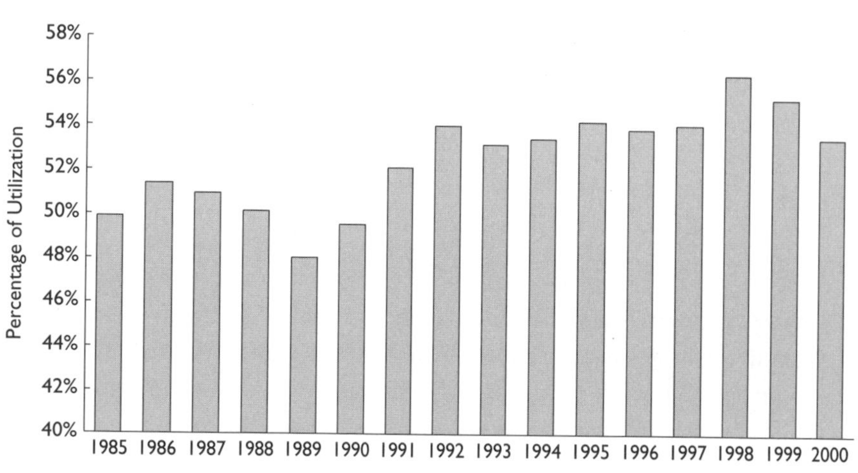

Source: Data from Department of Trade and Industry (2001).

Reserve Margin and Demand Growth in the UK, 1986-2000

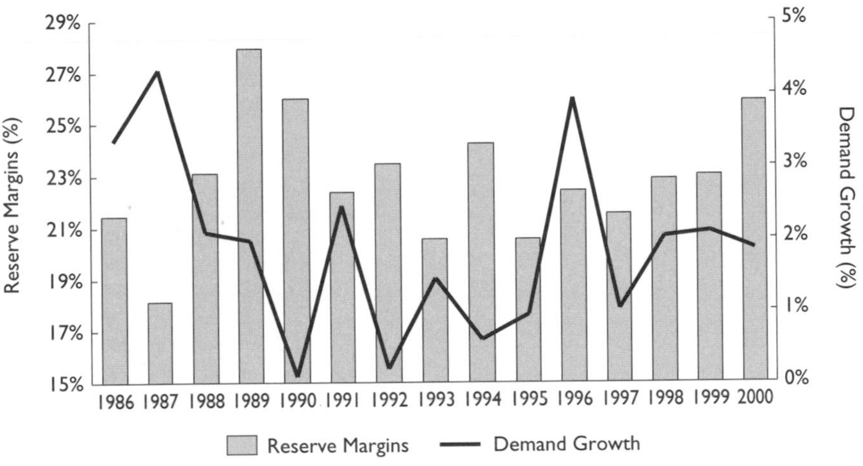

Source: Data from Department of Trade and Industry (2001).

The British generation mix, which was dominated by coal and to a lesser extent by oil and nuclear in the mid-1980s, is now more diversified, relying mainly on gas, coal, and nuclear.

As a result of the gas moratorium, some 17 projects amounting to 5.8GW of capacity have been refused approval to build. Another 27 projects amounting to 3.4GW of new capacity have received consent, including 22 CHP schemes[47]. Several new CCGT schemes were delayed as a result of the policy.

The UK now enjoys a healthy diversity in generation by historical standards, with coal, gas and nuclear all playing significant roles. But this trend to diversification would go in reverse should the 'dash' for gas continue. The exact growth rate of gas market share remains uncertain, yet gas has definitely been the fuel of commercial choice for new capacity.

47. *DTI (2000), Energy Report.*

Figure 17

Generation Mix in the UK, 1985-2000

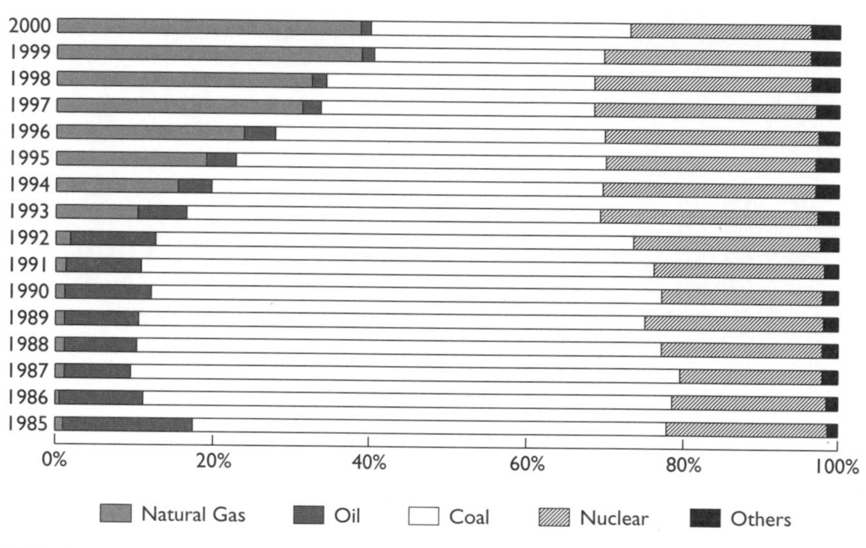

Source: Data from Department of Trade and Industry (2001).

Figure 18

Wholesale Prices and Generation Capacity Change, 1990-2000

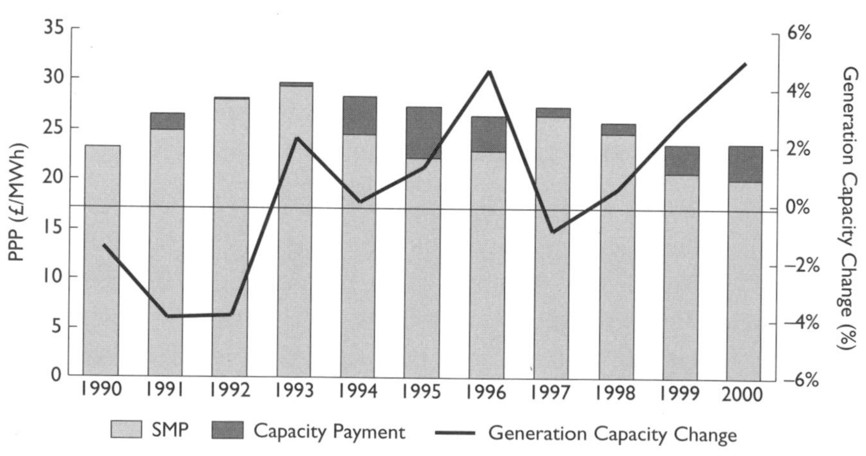

Source: Data from Logica ESIS' website.

Electricity prices in the household and industry sectors have fluctuated since privatisation, but all classes of consumers now pay less for electricity in real terms (excluding tax) than they did in 1990. Electricity prices to end users, however, are not a reliable indicator of efficiency improvements in power generation, since they incorporate transportation, distribution and retailing costs.

Wholesale prices are more significant as far as investment in electricity generation is concerned. Whilst prices in the Pool started at a low level, they rose steadily until 1993/94 and then decreased slightly. In the whole period, however, wholesale prices were generally considered above the cost of entry for potential developers, estimated to range from £17/MWh to £20/MWh for CCGT capacity at a 90 per cent load factor[48].

Figure 19

Retail Electricity Price in the UK, 1985-2000

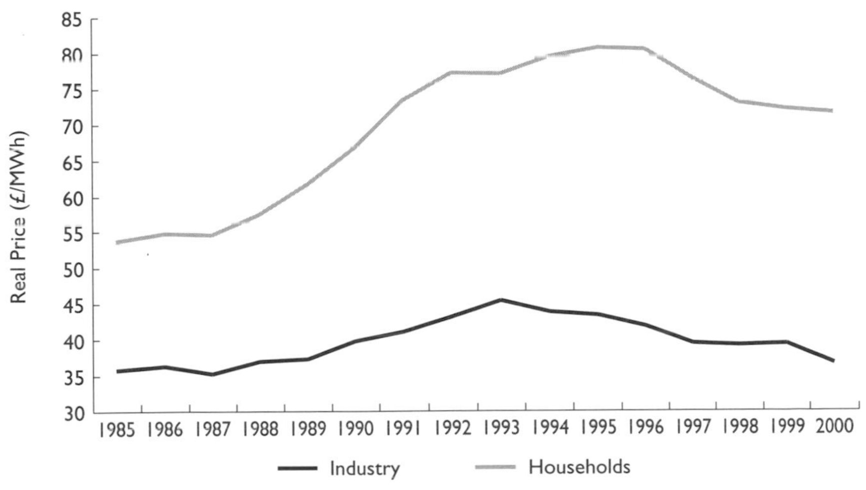

Source: Data from Department of Trade and Industry (2001).

48. *This estimation is taken from OFGEM, as reported in Competition Commission (2000). The regulator based its statements on reports by Merrill Lynch and CSFB.*

Assessment

After ten years of competition, investment has continued to flow into the British electricity supply industry and reserve margins remain relatively high. Following on a CEGB target of 24 percent in the pre-competitive era, reserve levels have moved in the range of 20 to 26 per cent through the 1990s.

The technology mix has changed considerably in the last 15 years. Coal has been gradually replaced by natural gas as the underlying economics made gas more competitive. The result has been increased fuel diversity even though investment has been concentrated in just one fuel. This suggests that the actual impact of competition on diversity depends on the initial position of each system.

Relatively high prices in the wholesale market, compared to the cost of entry, appear to be one of the main determinants of the system's satisfactory investment performance. The finding that prices are a key determinant of investment decisions conforms to expectations. Capacity payments have been volatile and prone to manipulation, and it is unlikely that they have played a major role in promoting investment.

There have been no significant barriers to entry into the generation sector, apart from a temporary government policy on granting consent for CCGT plant – the so-called gas moratorium. The authorisation procedure for new power plants in the UK is complex but apparently predictable. It did not discourage entry into generation.

Regulatory risk has been arguably high at various times during the 1990s. At various points, the regulator threatened to take remedial action against oligopolistic behaviour. There has also been considerable uncertainty in the last few years about the change of regulation and the introduction of NETA. But, regulatory risk does not seem to have had a noticeable impact on investment, which remained strong all over the period.

This UK experience contrasts with allegations that regulatory risk has been a deterrent of investment in other systems, including California. The UK experience casts some doubts on the role that regulatory risk may have actually played in other systems.

The Nordic Market: Norway and Sweden

The Norwegian electricity market was opened to competition in 1991. The market was subsequently extended to Sweden in 1996. More recently, Finland and Denmark entered NordPool. This section reviews the experience of Norway and Sweden. Integration of these two markets is strong, and for many purposes they can be considered a single market. There are common marketplaces for electricity as well as harmonised pricing and regulatory policies for their national grids.

■ Structure of the Industry

Industry Reforms Since the Early 1990s

Norway

Electricity market reform in Norway brought the full opening to competition of the generation and retail markets. Customers of all sizes were allowed to choose their supplier, although switching could be conditional upon a financial charge. This fee was discontinued for small customers in 1998 when load profiling – the use of average consumption patterns to determine individual consumption in between metered measurements – was introduced.

Unlike in the UK, Norway's reforms did not entail a radical restructuring of the electricity supply industry. The Energy Act 1991 introduced a distinction between the generation market, which was liberalised, and transportation functions, which were to remain regulated. The state electricity authority was split into a production company – Statkraft – and a system operator for the high-voltage grid – Statnett SF. There was no major change in the ownership structure

Table 8

Existing Interconnections in 2000

Countries	Maximum transmission capacity (MW)	
Norway – Sweden(1)	To Norway: 3,495	To Sweden: 4,545
Norway – Finland	To Norway: 100	To Finland: 100
Norway – Denmark	To Norway: 1,040	To Denmark: 1,040
Norway – Russia	To Norway: 50	To Russia: 50
Sweden – Finland(2)	To Sweden: 2,130	To Finland: 1,530
Sweden – Denmark(3)	To Sweden: 2,680	To Denmark: 2,640
Sweden – Germany	To Sweden: 600	To Germany: 600
Sweden – Poland	To Sweden: 600	To Poland: 600
Finland – Russia	To Finland: 1,160	To Russia: 60
Denmark – Germany	To Denmark: 1,950	To Germany: 1,950
Norway – Rest of the World	To Norway: 4,685	From Norway: 5,735
Sweden – Rest of the World	To Sweden: 10,555	From Sweden: 8,865

(1) Thermal limit for Ofoten-Ritsem stations (1,350 MW) and Røssåga-Aujore stations (415 MW); stability problems and generation in nearby power plants may lower the limit. In addition, the transmission capacity can in certain situations be lower owing to bottlenecks in the Norwegian and Swedish networks.

(2) In certain situations, the transmission capacity can be lower than the limit given here.

(3) Thermal limit on three stations amounting to 1,500 MW from Sweden and 900 MW to Sweden; the total transmission capacity is 1,775 MW to Denmark and 1,700 MW to Sweden.

Source: Nordel (2001).

of the ESI, which largely remained in public hands. Furthermore, the different owners of the grid were required to allow third-party access at a regulated tariff. Companies involved in generation and transmission or distribution were required to unbundle their activities, but only on an accounting basis.

A voluntary market for physical and financial contracts was created in Norway at the time of reform. With the incorporation of Sweden this power exchange was transformed into NordPool. Although participation in the spot market is optional, the market provides a widely used reference price. For most customers, electricity charges are based entirely on actual spot market prices. In 2000, more than a quarter of total consumption of electricity in the Nordic countries was sold in the NordPool physical market.

Sweden

Swedish reforms of 1996 followed the Norwegian model. Electricity generation and supply were liberalised, whilst a system of regulated third-party access to the network was introduced. All customers were allowed to choose their supplier. From 1999, they have incurred no cost in switching suppliers since the demand to install meters with hourly metering capability was abolished.

Before the reform, each of the Nordic countries aimed at being self-sufficient in electricity, even if some electricity was imported. A smaller need for expanding generation capacity has been perceived after 1996, as the volume of trade has increased. The two countries have strong interconnections, as well as connections with other countries.

Current Industry Structure

There have been no major changes in the structure of the industry since market reform started. The main trend has been structural integration of Nordic companies through acquisitions, mergers and co-operation agreements within the NordPool and beyond it. This process of structural transformation has resulted in a less fragmented electricity supply industry. It has yielded some more efficient and rational units as initially the industry had been highly atomised, but it has also increased the size of some of the largest players.

The Norwegian power industry is characterised by a very fragmented supply structure with numerous small generating companies. A total of 160 companies are engaged in electricity generation, of which less than a third do generation only, the rest being also engaged in distribution and trading. In 1995, there were 39 major power producers, with the ten largest accounting for about 66 per cent of installed capacity. The state-owned company Statkraft accounts for just under one-third of hydropower generation. It owns 113 water reservoirs, with an aggregate maximum capacity of approximately 33.7 TWh, or almost 40 per cent of Norway's total reservoir capacity.

In Sweden there are six major power producers vertically integrated into distribution and trading activities, around 224 distribution companies, which typically own some power generation assets, and 215 electricity trading companies[49]. However, electricity generation within Sweden is more highly concentrated than it would seem at first sight. In 2000, the two largest generators produced about two thirds of total output. This has resulted from a wave of mergers and acquisitions during the last fifteen years, which still continues. In 1999, the third and fourth largest Swedish generators, Gullspångs Kraft and Stockholm Energi, merged into Birka Energi.

The concentration of generation in the NordPool area is lower. The two largest producers in Norway and Sweden accounted altogether for around 27 per cent of Nordic electricity generation in 2000 and, apart from Vatenfall, none of them accounted for more than 10 per cent. Whether the relevant market for competition is the whole NordPool region or parts of it depends on changing demand and supply conditions. During peak periods, these conditions may result in congested transmission links which limit the geographical scope of competition in generation. This is reflected in differences between spot electricity prices in the two countries during certain periods. When such differences occur, the relatively high concentration of ownership of generation, in particular within Sweden, raises concerns that firms may be using their market power to raise prices.

Contrary to the United Kingdom, the market reform process has not brought privatisation of the power industry. In Norway, the government owns the largest electricity producer, Statkraft,

49. *Distribution activities are required by law to be managed by separate legal entities and are not allowed to engage in other electricity supply industry activities.*

Table 9

Largest Nordic Electricity Generators in 2000

	Electricity generated	Proportion in Nordic countries	Proportion in their domestic market
Norway	*142.8 TWh*	*37 %*	
Statkraft	40.2 TWh	10 %	28 %
Norsk Hydro	11.5 TWh	3 %	8 %
Sweden	*141.9 TWh*	*37 %*	
Vatenfall	63.9 TWh	18 %	45 %
Skydraft	27.2 TWh	7 %	19 %

Note: Nordic countries encompass Norway, Sweden, Finland, and Denmark.
Source: Swedish National Energy Administration (2001).

and in total it owns about one third of the country's total generation capacity. The remainder remains largely in public hands, with municipalities owning slightly less than 60 per cent of Norway's electricity generation capacity.

Through the public company Statnett, the state also owns 76% of the central high-voltage grid. The company is also responsible for managing the entire national grid as well as interconnections with other countries. The remainder of the grid is owned by numerous private companies, counties and municipalities and hence its use is rented by Statnett, which entails excess administrative costs[50].

In Sweden, ownership of electricity generation assets is mixed. Government holds slightly less than half of generation assets through Vattenfall. The remainder is owned by municipalities (23 per cent), foreign utilities (17 per cent), and independent Swedish investors (around 10 per cent). In addition, the state owns Svenska Kraftnät (SK)[51], the company in charge of system operation, including the balance service, and transmission.

50. *Statnett has planned to increase its ownership of the grid in order to alleviate the situation.*

51. *SK was spun-off from Vattenfall in 1992. Cf. IEA (2001).*

Institutional Structures

Both countries share a common approach to institutional structures based on: (i) delegating most regulatory tasks to a ministerial agency hierarchically responsible to government but endowed with some degree of independence in the management of day-to-day regulatory affairs; and (ii) a relatively light-handed regulatory style in which some key decisions are reviewed (as opposed to made) by the regulatory authorities.

Norway

In Norway, there are three main actors in electricity regulation: the Ministry of Petroleum and Energy, the Water Resources and Energy Directorate (NVE), and the Competition Authority (NCA). Ultimate responsibility for regulation lies with the Ministry of Petroleum and Energy which is also responsible for setting energy policy.

NVE administers water and energy resources. It is a subordinated ministerial agency whose decisions can be revised by the Ministry of Petroleum and Energy but it is meant to be independent in day-to-day affairs. Its functions cover a broad spectrum of regulatory activities, including the licensing of electric activities and market regulation. Economic regulation of the Norwegian electricity market is the responsibility of the Energy and Regulation Division of the NVE.

The regulation division prepares the Master Plan for Water Resources, conducts surveys of electricity production and consumption, co-ordinates regional and national grid planning, and assesses and licences plans for electricity production plants and district heating. It reports, along with other divisions, to the director general who, in turn, is subordinate to the Ministry of Petroleum and Energy. The ministry is both the owner of a substantial part of the electricity sector and the final arbiter of regulatory decisions taken on appeal.

NVE and NCA have overlapping competence to apply and enforce competition rules. Under an informal agreement between the two agencies, however, NVE has sole responsibility to intervene against anti-competitive behaviour that is not covered by the prohibitions of the Competition Act. The two agencies issued a joint report in 1996 on the delineation of competencies; it provides for parallel action in merger and anti-competitive behaviour cases, and it establishes some co-ordination and consultation mechanisms between them.

Sweden

In Sweden, there are three main institutional actors: the Ministry of Industry, Employment and Communications, the Swedish National Energy Administration (NEA), and the Competition Authority. Lead responsibility for regulation lies with the ministry. The Swedish parliament, the Riksdag, has also played a key role in some key energy policies, notably plans to phase out nuclear plants.

In 1998, NEA was set up to replace the energy-policy functions of the National Board for Industrial and Technical Development. NEA monitors the electricity market and provides analyses of the links among energy, the environment and economic growth.

Responsibility for regulating the network resides with the Office of the Electricity and Gas Regulator, which is part of NEA. The office may request information that is required for the purposes of supervision. Such a request may be backed by a penalty in case of non-compliance. The overall regulatory approach is based on limited regulatory intervention[52].

The Competition Authority applies competition rules and monitors the competitive conditions of production and trading in electricity. The authority has given the Office for the Electricity and Gas Regulator assistance in following the development of

52. The network authority monitors tariffs and has the power to accept or reject modifications proposed by the network companies.

market conditions. The government or the office regularly invites the Competition Authority to submit its views on reports.

The integration of different national electricity markets in Nord Pool has required international co-operation among regulatory authorities in such matters as approving rules for organised markets, transmission tariffs and exchange of information. System operators have co-operated through Nordel, which is a forum for technical co-operation between system operators.

■ Entry and Investment

Investment and System Development Process

Norway

In Norway, entry into the market for electricity generation is governed by an authorisation procedure which is particularly strict as regards the use of hydropower resources. The requirements to obtain licences are detailed in an extensive legislative framework.

The right to award licences for the construction of electrical facilities lies with NVE. Its decisions can be appealed to the Ministry of Petroleum and Energy. Applications for licences are processed by several authorities in addition to NVE such as the Storting (parliament) and the ministry. The authorities ensure that hydropower resources are used as effectively as possible, while minimising environmental impact. The Master Plan for Water Resources sets out priorities for considering individual hydropower projects, based on economic considerations and possible conflicts with other interests. An environmental assessment is made on proposed projects, and there is a public consultation process where stakeholders are extensively heard.

Several regulatory constraints apply to investment, many designed to protect the environment. Possible expansion of gas-fired power generation has been the subject of discussion and uncertainty for a number of years. A moratorium on large-scale hydro development was imposed in January 2001.

Norway has provided subsidies for wind power through investment and operation grants. The grants absorb half of the Norwegian electricity tax. Investment grants are awarded to wind farms with total installed capacity above 1,500 kW and in which every unit has a rating of 500 kW or more. These grants amount to 25 per cent of the costs.

Following the 1999 White Paper on energy policy, the government decided to reorganise the national energy-efficiency scheme. It set up a new government body, ENOVA, to reorganise energy use and production. The objective is to increase the amount of electricity generated from new renewable sources so that wind power and CHP would become a larger part of overall energy production. ENOVA will be financed by a new fund of $60.5 million the first year.

Sweden

In Sweden, entry into generation is subject to an authorisation procedure that does not contain any energy-specific criteria. In addition to the framework set up by the 1996 Energy Act, a number of government policies influence the industry. Two Parliamentary decisions, adopted in 1991 and 1997, set guidelines for the future development of energy policy. In particular, they set guidelines for electricity generation capacity and establish subsidies and other support measures to promote energy efficiency, and the development of renewable energy sources.

Sweden has a long-standing political commitment to phase out nuclear power. In 1980, the government declared that nuclear power was to be phased out at a rate compatible with electrical power requirements for the maintenance of employment and national well-being. The recommended date for closing the last reactor is no later than 2010. Following a parliamentary commission report in 1997, guidelines for energy policy were set down in the Sustainable Energy Supply Bill, which complemented earlier guidelines in the 1991 Energy Policy Bill. The shut down of two nuclear reactors at Barsebäck was scheduled for 1 July 1998 and 1 July 2001[53] respectively. But the previous commitment to closing Sweden's last nuclear reactor no later than 2010 was revoked. In fact, the first Barsebäck reactor was closed in November 1999. The second reactor at this station will be shut down only if the resulting loss of capacity can be compensated by new generation capacity and by reduced consumption of electricity. In October 2000, the government decided that the conditions for shutting down Barsebäck 2 were not met, but that they ought to be met by the end of 2003. The future of the remaining nuclear reactors remains uncertain.

An extensive energy policy programme with total funding of $887 million is being implemented in order to reduce the costs of the use of renewables so as to make them economically viable alternatives to nuclear power and fossil fuels.

Sweden offers substantial financial support for renewable electricity generation. Grants have been awarded for nine plants with a total output of 164 MW and an estimated annual generation of 0.84 TWh which will be commissioned from 2000 to 2003. New wind power units are subsidised through an investment grant and an operation grant corresponding to the electricity tax in southern Sweden. Finally, a grant is given to small-scale plants, i.e. plants with an output below 1,500 kW.

Main Constraints on Investment

Norway

Norway's energy policy imposes severe constraints on the construction of new electricity generation capacity. The expansion of hydro capacity, virtually the only source of electricity in Norway, has been restricted because of environmental

53. *IEA (2001); Swedish National Energy Administration (2001).*

concerns. Most of the country's potential hydro resources have been developed and a substantial part of the remainder (about 20 per cent) is protected against development for environmental reasons. The planned hydropower expansion in Beiarn, which was licensed at the end of the 1980s, was halted on political grounds in the autumn of 2000, just when work should have commenced.

On 1 January 2001, the prime minister announced that there would be no more new large-scale hydropower developments in the country, as most of the remaining potential sites are located in protected environment areas and/or face opposition for its development by various civil society groups.

Investment in gas-fired generation – to take advantage of Norway's offshore natural gas resources – has been hobbled by regulatory and political uncertainty as to future environmental standards, which may alter the projects' profitability. Since 1996, licences have been issued for the construction of gas-fired power plants, which are to generate 12 TWh annually once on-line.

Although three gas-fired power plants have received licences – at Kollsnes, Kårstø, and Skogn – none of the companies awarded licences has taken any final decision about the start-up of these projects. Conditions on emissions were set by the Ministry of the Environment in 2001.

In 2000, the government lost a vote of confidence on the natural gas power issue – over a proposal to allow the development of plants, but at the condition that plant's CO2 emissions were reduced by 90 per cent and its NOx emission by 80 per cent – and consequently resigned. Regulations were later amended to remove restrictions on carbon dioxide emissions from gas-fired power plants and to ensure that Norwegian producers meet the same regulations as do other EU producers. Norway's emission targets, however, could only be met by emission-reduction technology or regional trading in emissions. The criteria for emissions from gas-fired plants are expected to apply until an international quota system for greenhouse gases is established.

The Norwegian government encourages the development of wind energy, as there are many suitable sites along its coast but various organisations oppose wind energy.

Sweden

In Sweden, the main constraints on investment in power generation concern hydro resources. The development of hydropower is limited by a Parliamentary decision banning further exploitation of "national rivers" and other hydro resources. Complex and, in some instances, uncertain energy policies on the phase out of nuclear power and its replacement with renewables may have increased regulatory risk in the eyes of potential investors.

■ Market Design

In the Nordic wholesale market, electricity is either traded bilaterally between market players, or else in the markets organised by NordPool. Physical trade between Norway, Sweden and Finland, and between Norway and Denmark, takes place in the spot market. NordPool consists of two physical markets, called Elspot and Elbas. Elspot is the market for trading electricity for delivery the following day. Prices are determined for each hour throughout the day, on the basis of the quantity of electricity that participants announce that they will be buying and selling. Elbas, launched in 1999, is a continuous physical market where electricity is traded up to two hours before delivery. This market is only available to Swedish and Finnish participants, and is not used by the Norwegian system operator. In Norway, Statnett organises a separate market to adjust power generation and consumption at short notice. Nord Pool also organises financial markets for participants to hedge prices and manages the commercial risk they face.

The geographical scope of the electricity market changes depending on demand conditions. Large price differences occur during certain time periods when there is congestion in the transmission system. When this occurs, high seller concentration within the Swedish market could result in anticompetitive prices.

Prices in NordPool are below entry cost for new generators, which is evaluated at a minimum of 25 to 30 NOK/MWh. Low prices have been a major factor in discouraging investment in power generation and seem to have contributed to the closure of some peaking plants in Sweden. Since 2000, prices have risen steadily in both Norway and Sweden, which has provoked public concern and led to investigations in the Swedish market. However, these 'high' prices are still considered to be below entry costs and hence they may not be enough to create incentives for electricity generation investment.

Performance

In Norway, demand for electricity has grown slowly but consistently in the last fifteen years, at an average 1.21 per cent per year. Generating capacity grew from 1986 to 1989 but stagnated in the first half of the 1990s. New additions took place from 1995 to 1997. Since then electric power generation capacity has been slightly reduced.

Figure 20

Generation Capacity and Demand in Norway, 1985-2000

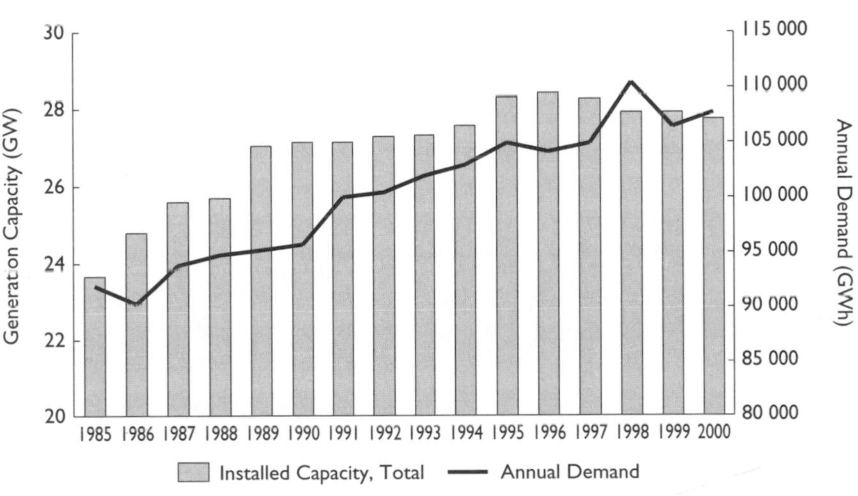

Source: Data from the International Energy Database and the national statistic administration.

Figure 21

Generation Capacity and Demand in Sweden, 1985-2000

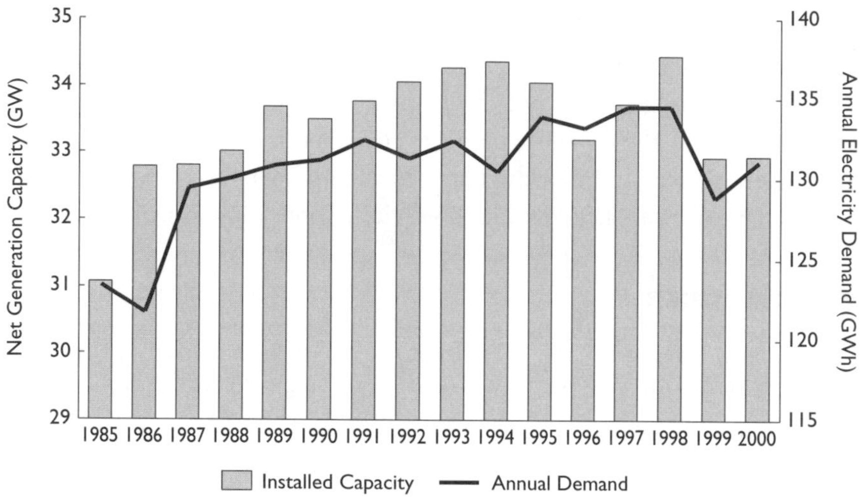

Source: Data from the International Energy Database and the national statistic administration.

Figure 22

Capacity Utilisation in Norway and Sweden, 1985-2000

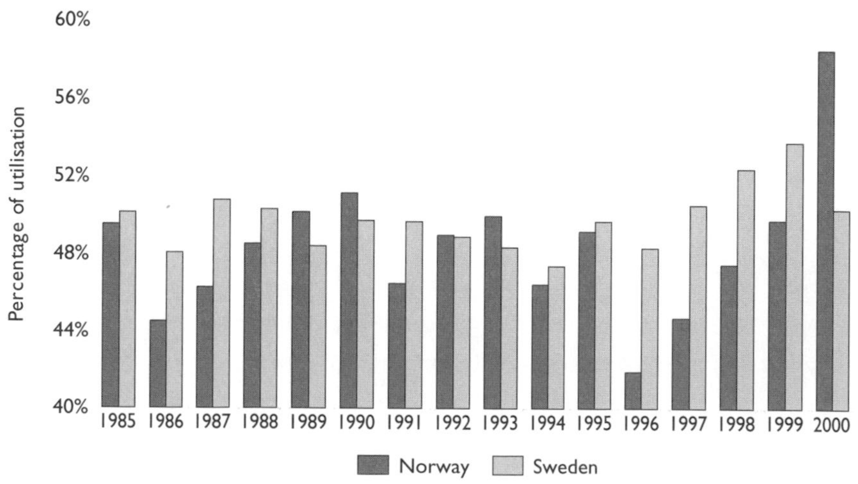

Source: Data from the International Energy Database and the national statistic administration.

In Sweden, demand for electric power has grown at a less regular pace, at rates averaging less than one per cent. After steady capacity additions until the mid-1990s, electricity generation capacity has fluctuated over the last decade. Demand decreased over the period. In the 1970s and early 1980s, new nuclear generating capacity met electricity demand growth and replaced oil, which was used both in power generation and heating. No additional nuclear capacity has been put on line since 1985. In the 1990s, oil-fired generating capacity continued to be decommissioned, including an additional 1,930 MW which were decommissioned in 1998. There has also been an increase in wind power and gas-fired generating capacity but their contribution to total electricity production remains very small.

Capacity utilisation – an indicator of capacity use efficiency – has fluctuated in the last fifteen years, with a slight overall increase, to around 50 per cent. Capacity utilisation fluctuates with water reserves, especially in Norway where virtually all electricity capacity relies on hydro.

The electricity fuel portfolio has been very different in the two countries. In Norway, generation is almost exclusively based on hydropower. Variations in output are largely due to fluctuations in rainfall. Electricity generated in Sweden is produced mainly from hydro and nuclear power plants, which accounted for 83 per cent of total production in 2000. Their respective contributions have changed over time: they were roughly similar until recent years but, following nuclear plant closure, there is now more hydro than nuclear power generation (53 per cent and 30 per cent, respectively, in 2000). The remaining electricity is produced by combined heat and power (CHP) plants, which generated around 10 per cent of total production in 2000 and, to a lesser degree, from oil condensing power, gas turbines and wind power.

In both Norway and Sweden, reserve margins have fluctuated widely over the last fifteen years, ranging between 24 and 37 per cent and 20 and 30 per cent respectively. Since regulatory reform took place, reserve margins have slightly declined to 29 per cent in Norway and 21 per cent in Sweden. However, reserve margins are less significant in a hydro system than in others.

Figure 23

Fuel Mix in Norway, 1985-2000

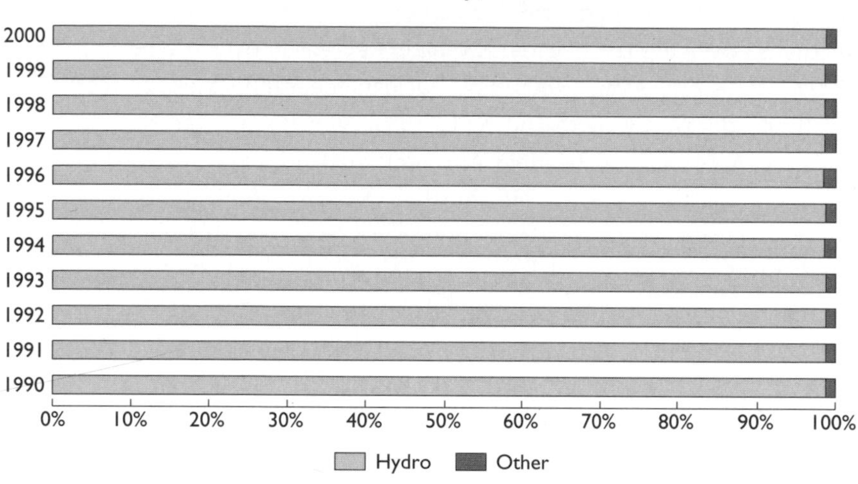

Source: Data from the International Energy Database and the national statistic administration.

Figure 24

Fuel Mix in Sweden, 1990-2000

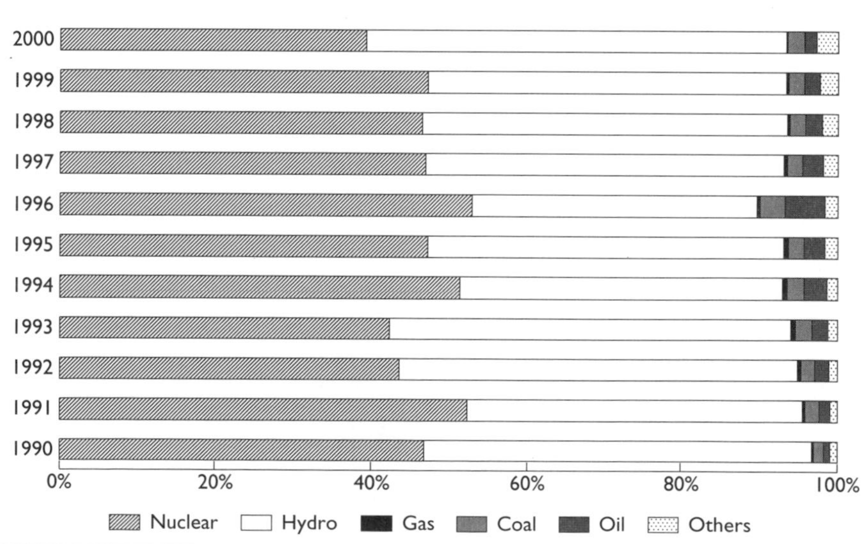

Source: Data from the International Energy Database and the national statistic administration.

Figure 25

Reserve Margins and Demand Growth in Norway, 1985-2000

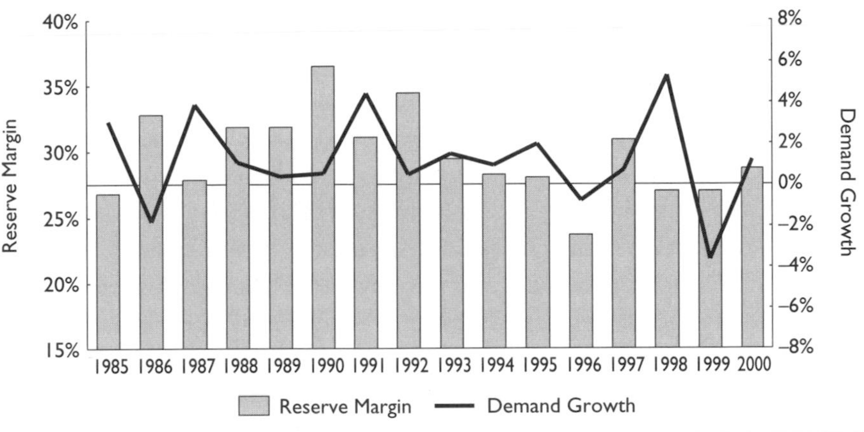

Source: Data from the International Energy Database and the national statistic administration.

Figure 26

Reserve Margins and Demand Growth in Sweden, 1985-2000

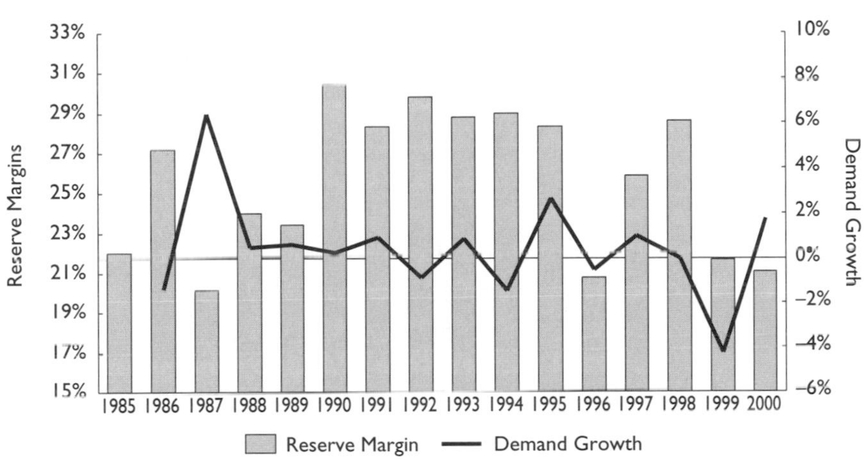

Source: Data from the International Energy Database and the national statistic administration.

Adequate reserve capacity is available in the Nordic power system during years of normal rainfall. But extremely low precipitation or lengthy cold spells can lead to a power shortfall.

Problems have been encountered with peaking capacity. Low prices have rendered some peaking units unprofitable. This problem has been particularly acute in Sweden. Electricity market reform eliminated contractual demands that the larger utilities should have stand-by generation capacity available. As a result, keeping gas turbine and oil-fired condensing power plants in service could no longer be commercially justified. Conventional thermal power capacity has shrunk in recent years and peaking capacity has been shrinking. To compensate, the power utilities have imported electricity from neighbouring countries.

In 1996 there were seven major condensing power plants with a total rating of about 2,820 MW. Today only one of these plants is available, with an output of 330 MW. During the autumn of 1999, Svenska Kraftnät decided to allocate contingency funds extending the utilisation of one unit of Karlashamn oil-fired power station until 2002. In addition, Svenska Kraftnät introduced a special price into its balance service for an assessed risk of power shortage which ranges between 3 and 9 SEK/kWh. The balance center companies — companies which supply extra electrical energy to the network when needed — will have to pay this price when they have a deficit on critical occasions.

In Norway, Statnett has entered into reserve output contracts with market players to ensure that there are sufficient immediately available reserves in the system. Until November 2000, Statnett reserved a certain amount of output on a daily basis if a power shortage was expected. Generators were paid not to report production on the spot market but instead to report this reserve output in the regulating power market. This system was replaced in November 2001 by reserve output contracts for three months or one year at a time. Reserve contracts comprise approximately 1,000 MW of production and 700 MW of consumption.

Figure 27

Spot Prices in NordPool, 1994-2001

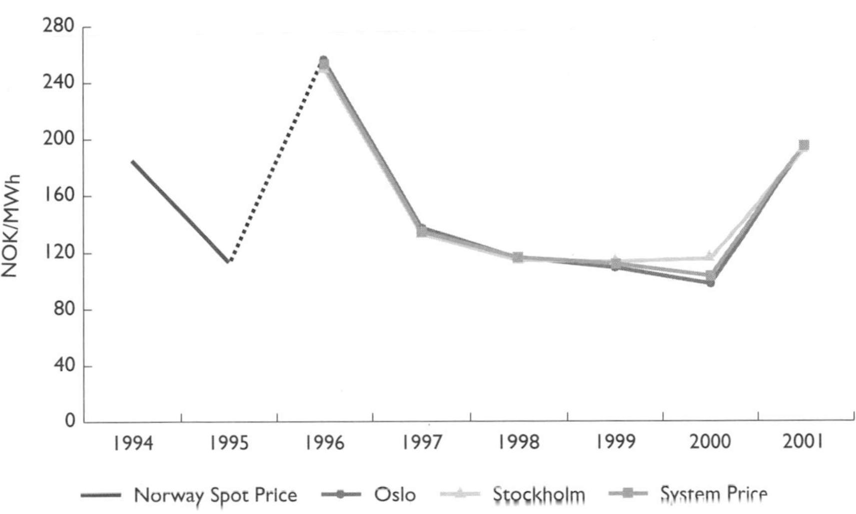

Source: Data from NordPool and the Norwegian Statistics Authorities.

Retail electricity prices in Norway and Sweden are very low by comparison to other countries. Prices are lower than in New Zealand, where electricity generation is also hydro-based and where competition has also been introduced, and also lower than in Finland and Denmark.

In 2001, prices rose in NordPool, and the rise has been reflected in retail prices. This has led to investigations in Sweden. The Norwegian Competition Authority calculates that between 1st January 2000 and 1st January 2001, the average weighted power price to households rose 11.9 per cent to 33.57 øre/kWh including, VAT and tax.

Assessment

Investment has been modest in Norway and Sweden over the last decade. This has actually resulted in a slight decrease in installed capacity in recent years. Reserve margins fell in Sweden in the years after liberalisation. They remain, however, at more than 20 per cent in both countries, although this is less significant in Norway because of its reliance on hydroelectricity.

A key factor explaining the weak investment performance is wholesale prices well below entry costs for new generation. Much new investment has been directed towards technologies which are eligible for subsidies. Low prices have been a particular problem for investment into peaking capacity. Seasonal and annual variations are very large depending on rainfall and winter temperatures.

Entry into the generation markets of Sweden and Norway is limited, particularly in Norway, by a significant number of policies and procedures that restrict the choice of technology and make obtaining authorisations difficult. However, policy constraints did not appear to play a major role in a context in which low prices rendered most investments unprofitable. Policy barriers to investment could become binding in a different context, should prices rise high enough to induce investment.

In Norway, investment in the sector is now a government concern. Work by Nordel illustrates the extent of the problem. The Nordic energy balance to 2005 is relatively strong, with an average net export from Scandinavia of around 5 TWh. In dry years, however, the balance is weak, resulting in considerable increases in forecast prices to ration available production. Of 13 TWh forecast imports in dry years, only about 9 TWh could be sourced from Scandinavian countries.

The remainder would have to come from elsewhere in Europe. Without cables between Norway and the continent, Nordel estimates that Norwegian prices in dry years would rise to around four times the average annual price. Nordel's study also shows the importance of back-up capacity in the Nordic market. Nordel concludes that the risk of loss of load in the Nordic system can no longer be regarded as negligible.

Australia: the National Electricity Market

■ Structure of the Industry

Industry Reforms Since the Mid-1990s

In Australia, the electricity industry was traditionally organised by state. Interstate grid connections were weak, and electricity trade between interconnected states was limited. Electricity reforms have occurred both at the state and national levels. At national level the aim was to develop a national electricity market (NEM) for the wholesale supply and purchase of electricity in five Australian states and territories – Victoria, New South Wales (NSW), the Australian Capital Territory (ACT), Queensland, and South Australia (SA). The market provides open access to transmission and distribution networks by generators, retailers and customers, co-ordinated planning of the interconnected power systems of the NEM jurisdictions and maintenance of system security.

At the state level, reform was led by the two most populous states: Victoria, which privatised and restructured its electricity sector in 1994, and New South Wales (NSW), which established a daily pool in 1996. The National Electricity Market was launched in May 1997 in Victoria, New South Wales, and the Australian Capital Territory. This was called NEM1. Since then, NEM has gradually extended to other states. South Australia entered the market in December 1998. Queensland established an interim stand-alone competitive market in January 1998, but only became physically part of the NEM in early 2001 on completion of the interconnector to New South Wales. Tasmania is expected to be interconnected to the NEM in 2002, through the Basslink interconnector.

Australia has adopted a gradual approach to introducing retail competition, with schedules differing from one state to the other. The ultimate aim is that all electricity consumers can choose their electricity retailers, but the dates for this remain uncertain.

Current Industry Structure

Prior to reform, the industry consisted of vertically integrated state-owned companies that served each of the states. Reform resulted in industry restructuring, notably through splitting up the electrical industries along functional lines and the creation of several generation companies in each of the states. Victoria and Queensland reforms also included privatisation.

In 1993/94, the State Electricity Commission of Victoria was separated into three segments — generation, transmission, and distribution, with the intention of privatising it. The generation sector was split among five companies and the Victorian power exchange was established to operate the wholesale power generation market. The transmission sector was divided into two components. PowerNet Victoria owned the high voltage transmission grid and was made responsible for its maintenance; and the Victorian Power Exchange was made responsible for pool operations and system dispatch.

In New South Wales, generation and transmission assets were separated into corporatised state-owned entities. Pacific Power owned a total of 11,515 MW of generating capacity (excluding the Snowy Mountains Hydroelectric Scheme's generation), about 32 per cent of the country's power generation capacity. The management, operation and maintenance of the state's high-voltage transmission grid became the responsibility of TransGrid. The Snowy Mountains Hydroelectric Scheme (SMHES) is a co-operative venture between the Australian Commonwealth Government, New South Wales and Victoria. It sells power to the central government and the electricity distributors in both states where it represents a vital part of supply arrangements. It has generating capacity of about 3,740 MW, over 10 per cent of the country's total capacity. Prior to completion of the NEM, the Scheme was corporatized. It has since sold electricity on the national grid in competition with other state and interstate generators.

The Australian Capital Territory, which consists of Canberra and surrounding areas, corporatized its electricity industry in 1995, after separating it from water and sewage functions. The state does not generate its own electricity and hence must rely on imports from New South Wales and the Snowy Mountain Hydroelectric Scheme.

In Queensland, the state Electricity Commission was restructured and corporatized in 1995 as two government corporations: AUSTA Electric, responsible for electricity generation, and the Queensland Transmission and Supply Corporation (QTSC), responsible for retail supply, distribution, and transmission. AUSTA Electric was split into three generating companies and partially privatised in 1997. Since that time the government no longer controls either electricity prices or the enterprise's investment plans. In South Australia, the vertically integrated state-owned utility, Electricity Trust of South Australia, was restructured and corporatised in 1995 as ETSA Corporation. The latter has four subsidiaries, among which ETSA Generation is responsible for generation and ETSA Transmission is in charge of transmission, system control, and system planning.

Table 10

Overview of Generation Market Structure, 1999

	Largest generator	Two largest generators
Victoria	31 %	54 %
New South Wales	38 %	70 %
Queensland	27 %	54 %
South Australia	31 %	62 %

Source: IEA (2001).

Development of the transmission network is an essential part of reforms. Interconnections between the states have gradually been expanded, and further expansion is under way. For example, the Queensland-New South Wales Interconnector (QNI) was progressively placed in service in the last quarter of 2000[54]. However, connections between the different regions of the NEM remain modest. Exchanges among NEM regions amounted to only 7 per cent of total energy generated in the NEM in 1998/99. By way of comparison, international exchanges within the Nordic electricity market amounted to about 14 per cent of electricity generated in 1998.

Table 11

Interconnection and Trade within the NEM, 2000

	Maximum transmission capacity (MW)		Share of NEM generation(1)
Victoria – 'Snowy'	To Victoria: 1,500	To Snowy: 1,100	2%
Victoria – South. Australia	To Victoria: 250	To S.A.: 500	2%
NSW – 'Snowy'	To NSW: 2,150	To Snowy: 850	3%
NSW – Queensland (2)	To NSW: 500	To Queensland: 1,000	-

(1) 1998/99 figures.

(2) Operation started in early 2001.

Source: Australian Competition and Consumer Commission.

Institutional Structure

Many institutions participate in energy policy-making and regulation in Australia, in part because of the federal structure of the country. The states regulate the electricity industry while the Commonwealth government is in charge of interstate issues and economic management at the national level. The establishment of the NEM considerably modified the institutional landscape. An

54. Another example is the interconnection of Tasmania and Victoria, known as Basslink, which is currently under construction and will enable Tasmania to join the NEM by 2003, allowing hydro-generated electricity to be exported to the mainland at times of peak demand, while in off peak periods Victorian electricity could be sent across the Bass to Tasmania.

Table 12

Regulatory Agencies in the States and Territories

Victoria	Office of the Regulator-General
New South Wales	Independent Pricing and Regulatory Tribunal
Australian Capital Territory	Independent Pricing and Regulatory Commission
Queensland	Queensland Competition Authority
South Australia	South Australian Independent Industry Regulator

independent national electricity regulator was created – the Australian Competition and Consumer Commission (ACCC) – as well as a number of independent state regulators.

Most regulatory functions are performed by the independent regulatory agencies including: (i) promoting competition, (ii) maintaining an efficient and economic system, and (iii) protecting consumers' rights and interests. These agencies also issue licences for electricity companies operating in their region.

Figure 28

National Bodies Involved in the Regulation of the Electricity Market and their Main Functions

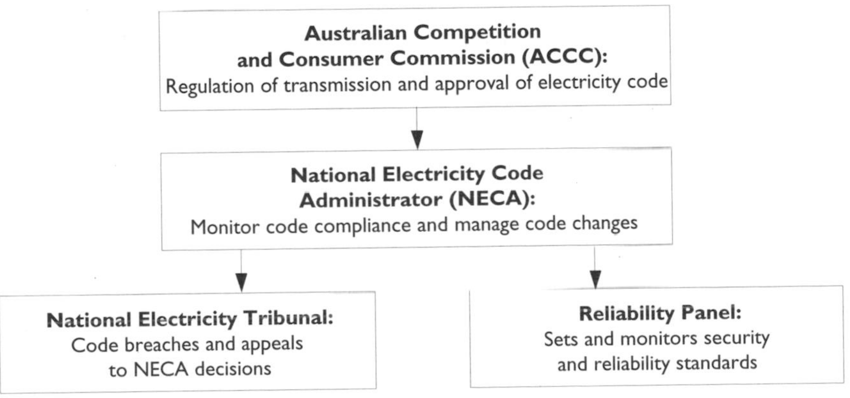

Source: IEA.

Alongside the state regulators, the national bodies involved in the regulation of the electricity market are the ACCC, the National Electricity Code Administrator (NECA), the National Electricity Tribunal and the Reliability Panel. The NEM operates under a detailed set of rules called the National Electricity Code. The National Electricity Market Management Company (NEMMCO) operates the power pool and related trading markets.

The ACCC is an independent statutory authority established in 1995 with responsibility for competition matters and third party access to facilities of national significance. It oversees transmission pricing, national electricity pricing and electricity market conduct. It also participates together with NECA in the approval of changes to the Electricity Code.

Specific regulatory responsibilities of the ACCC in the power industry relate to: (i) regulation of the network; (ii) organisation of the market; and (iii) promotion and defence of competition. The ACCC investigates market arrangements and behaviour that may contravene antitrust laws and evaluates electricity industry mergers.

NECA monitors compliance with the National Electricity Code and manages changes in the code. The National Electricity Tribunal intervenes when there are breaches of the code or appeals to NECA decisions. The Reliability Panel was established in 1997 and has a key role in system security and reliability.

The complexity of the institutional framework makes co-ordination between different regulatory bodies crucial. There have been some uncertainties about jurisdiction and potential overlap of functions. Recently, more frequent information exchanges have been developed among the different bodies involved in electricity regulation.

■ Entry and Investment

Investment and System Development Process

Prior to the establishment of NEM, the state governments were responsible for operational and planning activities. Together with the electricity industry in each state, they were accountable for supply reliability and system security. Investments in new generation or additional interconnection capacity were motivated by the need to maintain supply reliability in each region.

Since the establishment of the NEM, the initiative for investment in generation capacity has been left to potential developers. There is no formal planning of system development or monitoring of investment plans. The National Electricity Code includes a number of 'safety nets' to be used if the market fails to deliver acceptable supply reliability. These include the establishment of a Reliability Panel, charged with determining, on the advice of NEMMCO, a uniform reliability standard for the national market. In addition, the Panel has to establish guidelines for market intervention by NEMMCO, as a last resort to maintain reliability standards. NEMMCO can contract with market participants to procure generation and/or interruptible customer loads if the market fails to provide sufficient generating reserves. Since the creation of the NEM, an annual 'Statement of Opportunities' (SOO) has been prepared by NEMMCO to assess the need for additional capacity in the market over the next ten years. The SOO provides a brief summary of initiatives and projects which are expected to influence market development, including investment in generating capacity. NEMMCO's forecasts only consider 'committed' projects, where binding commercial decisions have been made.

The levels of supply reliability imposed by the Reliability Panel are similar to those which existed prior to the NEM. This standard is expressed as a maximum level of energy unsupplied because of a supply failure. It was set in 1998 at an annual average of 0.002 per cent of total energy consumed in the region.

Furthermore, the Reliability Panel set a minimum reserve level in each region which must be greater than or equal to the size of the largest single generating unit in that region. NEMMCO determines minimum reserves required to meet the Reliability Panel standards. It has also set guidelines for intervention in the market by NEMMCO acting as a reserve trader.

Table 13

Reserve Requirements in the National Electricity Market

NEM states	Minimum reserve level
Victoria	500 MW
New South Wales	660 MW
Queensland	350 MW[1]
South Australia	260 MW

[1] The minimum reserve level in Queensland was subject to a Code derogation. It has been assumed to increase from 350 MW to 420 MW for 2001and to 450 afterwards MW to keep pace with the increased size of the generating units installed as part of the Callide Power Plant, Millmerran Project, and Tarong North Project.

Source: NEMMCO (2001).

The construction of an electricity generating plant in Australia is subject to a licensing procedure at state level, usually by the state electricity regulator. In Victoria, for example, the licensing regime was set up by the Electricity Industry Act 1993. To be issued a generation licence, developers apply to the Office of the Regulator General. In practice, the main points considered by the Office are the technical capacity and the financial viability of the developer's project.

Main Constraints on Investment

There have been no major regulatory or policy constraints on investment in electricity generation. The Australian approach to regulatory reform has been intended to be 'light-handed'. The few constraints that exist are vesting arrangements, and the cap on spot prices. There have been, however, attempts by some states to favour certain technologies. Queensland plans to require generators to increase the share of gas-fired generation up to 15 per cent.

The development of the NEM has seen the implementation of vesting arrangements in New South Wales and South Australia. Generators and retailers make such arrangements to hedge the risk of a mismatch between the wholesale price of electricity, which fluctuates over time, and the regulated tariff. Tariffs set under this system do not reflect the spot price but rather the contracted price of energy. These contracts require authorisation by the ACCC.

On the other hand, the National Electricity Code has set a price cap. This is not only the maximum level at which generators can bid in the market but is also the price that is automatically triggered when NEMMCO orders an interruption of supply to regain balance in the system. The spot price is referred to as the 'Value of the Lost Load' (VoLL). It was originally set by the National Electricity Code at AU$5,000 per MWh. After the brownouts experienced in Victoria in February 2000 VoLL was increased to AU$10,000 per MWh in September 2001 and to AU$20,000 per MWh in April 2002. The change is intended to allow for both increased investment incentives and financial risk.

The ownership structure of the industry has sometimes been perceived as a continuing barrier to market access by foreign investors. The US International Trade Commission reported in 2000 that foreign investors found it difficult to compete with state-owned companies in New South Wales. These companies had low debts compared to privately financed plants and reportedly received support from the state government.

In addition, regulatory complexity — three national bodies, plus the state regulators — may have hindered investment since it created uncertainty and incurred extra costs for market players[55]. In addition, it is alleged that continuing legislative changes and amendments to the National Electricity Code have made corporate planning more difficult.

State governments have committed themselves to abating greenhouse gases through the National Greenhouse Strategy. In 2000, a mandatory goal was set for the use of renewable energy sources. To meet that goal requires a stronger growth of renewable

55. Four issues were raised in connection with the Australian regulatory structure in the US International Trade Commission 2000 Report. First, that there were not enough resources, skills, and experience in the field to staff so many separate regulatory agencies. Second, that the large number of regulators, with widely varying responsibilities, made it difficult to gain agreement on needed system reforms. Third, that it was possible for market participants to site their electricity assets in jurisdictions that provide the most favourable regulatory rulings. Last, that the different regulatory rules imposed by the state governments raised costs for those market players who operate nationally.

generating capacity. There are incentives for developers and generators to increase the use of renewable energy sources.

Market Design

NEM is structured around a common mandatory spot market for trading wholesale electricity that jointly manages system operation and dispatch. It is operated by the National Electricity Market Management Company (NEMMCO), which is owned by the participant states and the federal government, to which all generators with a capacity above 30 MW are obliged to sell their output.

The National Electricity Market determines a merit order for the dispatch of generation based on a five-minute cycle. The market clearing price for each half-hour trading period is calculated ex post as the time-weighted average of the six five-minute dispatch prices for that period. Market participants may hedge their risk by entering into long- and short-term financial contracts. A financial contracts market has developed in parallel to the NEM. Contracts for differences are traded bilaterally between parties. In addition, two electricity future contracts are traded in the Sydney Futures.

Performance

In Australia, electricity demand has grown at annual rates averaging 1.5 per cent in the NEM, ranging from less than 1 per cent in Victoria to 2.4 per cent in Queensland. New capacity was added mainly from 1993 to 1995 and in 1999, most of it in the states of Queensland and Victoria.

In the NEM, capacity utilisation has fluctuated in the last decade, yet always remained around 50 per cent. Whereas it was declining before 1995, capacity utilisation jumped to over 55 per cent in 1998 and remained just under 50 per cent in 1999.

Reserve margins have remained strong in the last decade, usually amounting to between 25% and 30% but they have receded since 1999. Larger demand growth in recent years has partly eliminated the excess generating capacity that existed at the beginning of

Figure 29

Installed Generation Capacity and Electricity Demand in the NEM, 1990-2000

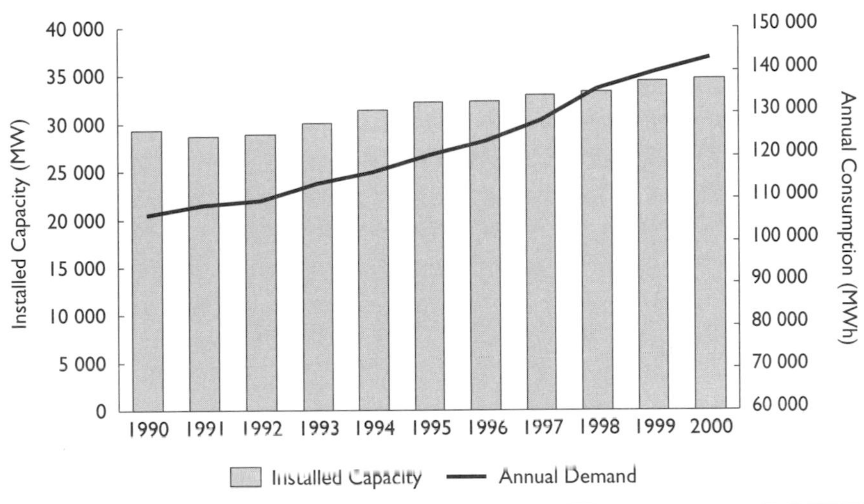

Source: Data from ESAA.

Figure 30

Generation Capacity in the NEM States (MW), 1990-2000

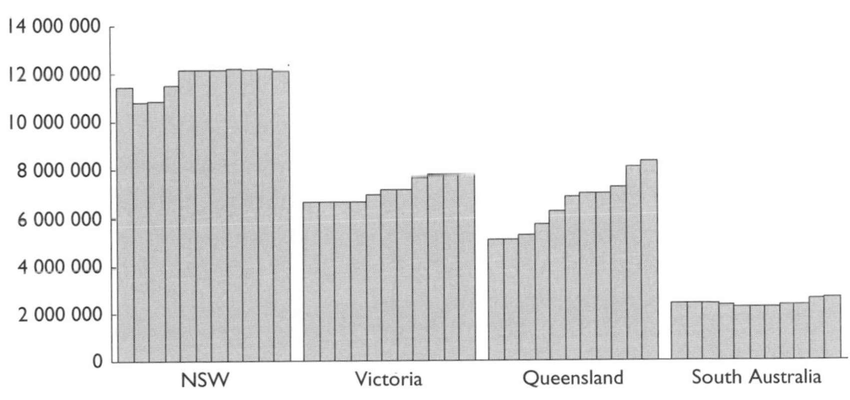

Source: Data from ESAA.

Figure 31

Capacity Utilisation in the NEM

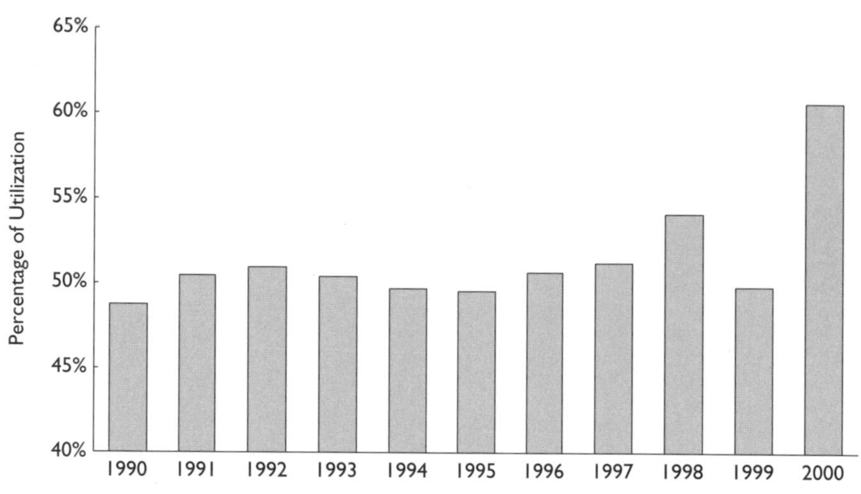

Source: Data from ESAA.

the 1990s[56]. The supply and demand balance varies by state. Reserves are low in New South Wales and South Australia and large in Queensland.

Both prices and investment performance have varied significantly across the states. Investment activity has been robust since NEM was established, with 1,695 MW of new capacity coming on line in the period 1998-2000 and 2,300 MW in additional capacity being constructed or committed. In addition, demand-side participation initiatives in Victoria and South Australia have achieved at least 143 MW of demand reduction. Resources have been allocated primarily towards the states where wholesale electricity prices have been relatively high, notably Queensland and South Australia.

In February 2000, Victoria faced a serious supply deficit that resulted in blackouts and other problems. The outages reflected a

56. In addition, average plant availability increased about 10 per cent from 1992 to 1999 to 93 per cent, thereby reducing the need for reserve capacity.

Figure 32

Reserve Margins in the NEM States (%), 1990-2000

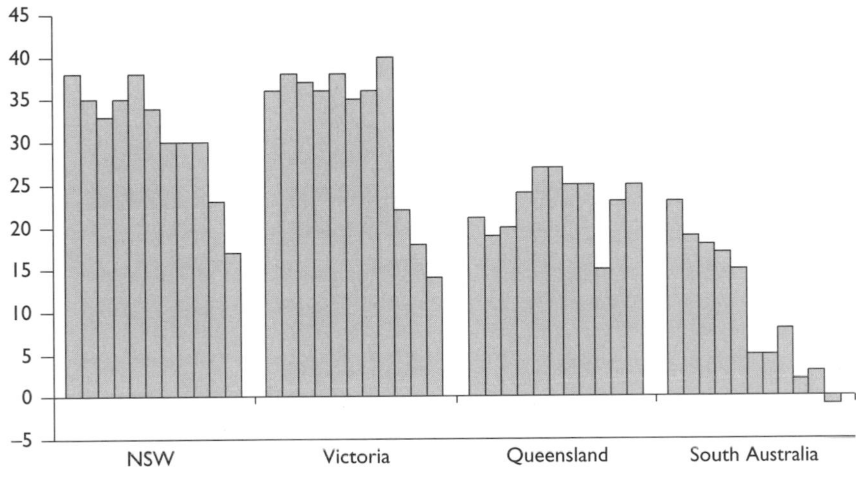

Source: Data from ESAA.

combination of unusual circumstances, including an industrial dispute, which took around 20 per cent of generating capacity off line, two unplanned generator outages and a heat wave across south-eastern Australia.

Since low-cost coal is abundant in Australia, electricity generation has mainly been provided through coal-fired power stations. Coal has accounted for about 80 per cent of the total fuel use. The remaining 20 per cent of electricity generation comes from gas-fired generation and hydroelectricity. The state of Tasmania, which may join the NEM in the future, is the exception; its electricity generation is mostly hydro based.

There are large price differences among the states reflecting different resource availability, demand configurations and government policies. Prices in the Victoria Pool dropped significantly in 1996 and have remained low on average in the NEM. Average annual prices in Victoria, for instance, dropped by more than half, from AU$28.1 per MWh in 1995 to AU$12.5 in 1997.

Figure 33

Average Electricity Retail Prices in Australia, 1989-2000

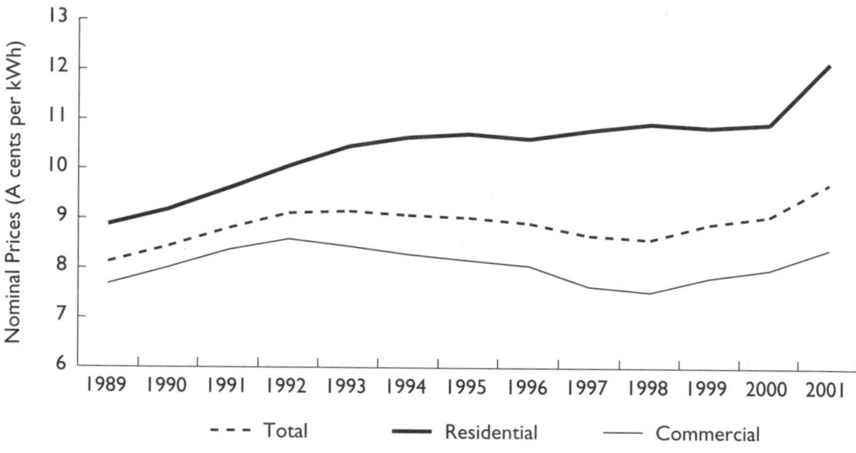

Source: Data from ESAA.

Figure 34

Total Average Electricity Retail Prices in NEM States, 1989-2001

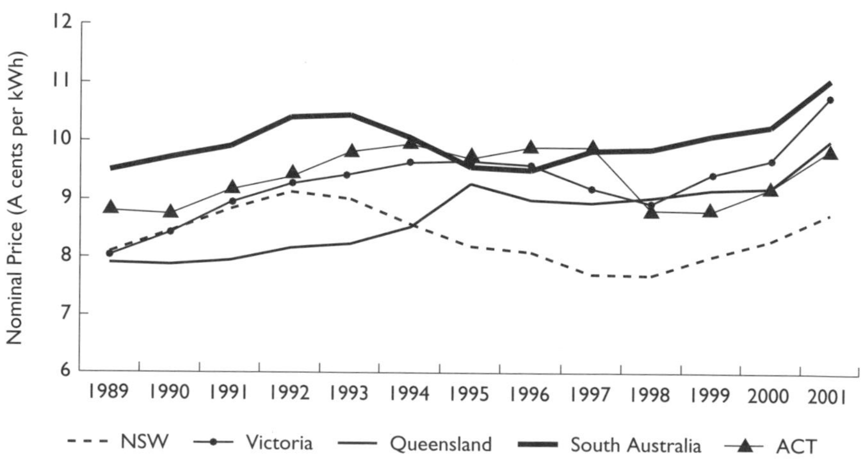

Source: Data from ESAA.

This trend seems to reflect both the onset of competition and the existence of large reserve margins of generation capacity in Australia. On the other hand, prices in Queensland and South Australia, where reserves are lower, have been much higher.

Prices have begun to rise recently, as increasing demand overtakes spare capacity. The spot prices in New South Wales and South Australia increased by 24 per cent and 28 per cent in 1999/2000 to averages of AU$30 per MWh and AU$69 respectively. Excluding the period of industrial disputes that resulted in a major drop of available capacity in Victoria in January and February of 2000, the increases amounted to about 16 per cent. Again excluding that atypical period, prices in Victoria remained broadly unchanged at AU$27 per MWh. Prices in Queensland fell by 18 per cent to AU$49 per MWh.

Assessment

From a starting point of strong reserve margins in the National Electricity Market, reserves dropped sharply from 1998 to 2000, although with large variations among states. Paradoxically, this drop has occurred despite stronger investment activity than in any of the other cases examined in this book, reflecting significant demand growth. The drop in reserves is consistent with the low prices observed in the initial years of NEM and underlying excess capacity. Investment activity could in turn be explained by high prices in some areas and the possibility of exporting to them. However, no clear conclusion can be drawn on how market forces have affected investment. In most states the market is very recent so that current investment results from decisions made before the market opened. Furthermore, state governments may have had an influence in investment decisions in those states where they remain the owners of electricity assets.

Additional generating capacity will be needed in the next few years to sustain reliability. Increasing wholesale prices, already observed in NEM, and developing interconnections should help to redress the balance. Current plans for new capacity suggest that investors are indeed increasingly active. Some uncertainties remain. The February 2000 power outages in Victoria, while largely the result of causes not related to market operation, indicate some vulnerability of the system.

Integration of NEM is still far from complete, as shown by sustained price differences among the NEM states. There is a need for further integration of the different state markets in the interest of reliability – some states have larger reserves than others but trade is limited by transmission constraints – and higher efficiency. Another recurrent issue concerns the role of some of the states as both owners and policy-makers, which may discourage potential investors.

California

■ Overview of the Electricity Crisis in California

Two years after reforming its electricity market, California went through an unprecedented power crisis. Wholesale electricity prices soared during 2000 and the first four months of 2001. Some utilities found themselves in an unsustainable financial position, and customers lost supply in a series of rolling blackouts. The California Power Exchange suspended trading on 30 January 2001 and filed for bankruptcy on 9 March 2001.

Many issues combined to create the problem in California. The state's market fundamentals *before* reform – tight supply and limited transmission capacity – made the system vulnerable. Flaws in the reform plan, such as retail price controls that muffled market signals, further weakened the system. Hurdles in the licensing process limited the ability of investors to react quickly enough to the sharp and unexpected growth in demand that occurred in 1999 and 2000. A series of unexpected one-off events concurred in the year 2000 to launch the crisis. These included very high gas prices, expensive

NOx emission permits, high power demand and a number of unexpected outages. Market instability was further aggravated by the anticompetitive behaviour of some market players.

The contribution of each of these factors to the crisis is still the subject of some debate. Our analysis indicates that barriers to investment created by inadequate authorisation processes played a major role in California's power crisis. Lengthy and unpredictable authorisation processes prevented the timely arrival of new capacity to compensate for the deteriorating reserve balance. Investment in generation peaked after such barriers to investment were removed.

The electricity crisis in California has sparked worldwide debate about electricity market reform. Is it working? How can it be taken forward successfully? How can the California problems be avoided elsewere? The California crisis stemmed from a combination of circumstances unlikely to recur elsewhere. But it highlighted some crucial lessons for reformers. It demonstrated that reform is not just about competition but also about reliable supply and adequate investment in generation and transmission. Reformers must design systems that further all these aims. Most important, reformed systems must provide clear price signals which enable market players to respond quickly and effectively to changing supply and demand.

Structure of the Industry

US Background

The current wave of electricity industry reforms in the United States started at the Federal level in the second half of the 1990s. A major part of the overall reform effort has been aimed at intensifying competition between power generators, mainly through provision of non-discriminatory access to the transmission grid. In 1996, the Federal Energy Regulatory Commission (FERC) issued wholesale open-access rules for wholesale trade requiring regulated third-party access to the network. Transmission owners are required to provide point-to point and network services under the same conditions they provide for themselves, and to separate their transmission and power-marketing activities.

In order to avoid discrimination in network access, FERC encourages, but does not mandate, the creation of so-called Regional Transmission Organisations (RTOs). This has resulted in the creation of four Independent System Operators (ISOs), one in California and three in the Northeast US, and plans to establish a large ISO covering twenty Midwest and Southwest states and the Canadian province of Manitoba. These entities manage and operate the transmission grid independently from the generators and other grid users, without necessarily owning the network.

New regulation focuses on levelling the playing field for supply competition by means of unbundling and transparency obligations imposed on the utilities. On the end-user side, it concentrates on enabling all consumers to choose their supplier and supporting consumer protection.

Electricity reforms in the United States have varied significantly across the states. Generally, the states with the highest electricity prices, such as California and the states in the Northeast have been the most active in trying to bring rates down. This chapter and the next consider two of these markets, California and PJM.

Industry Reforms

California was one of the first US states to restructure its electricity industry. Assembly Bill 1890, adopted in 1996, opened the entire retail market to competition in April 1998. Regulators adopted consumer-protection rules and standards of conduct for utilities. The reform involved divestiture of at least 50 per cent of generation by utilities and an allowance for recovery of stranded costs, financed by a competition transition charge. In addition, retail rates were to be frozen until full recovery of the stranded costs. Electricity tariffs were reduced by 10 per cent for all residential and small commercial customers.

Two new independent entities were set up, the California Power Exchange (CalPX) and the Independent System Operator (ISO). The latter operates the transmission network – which is still owned by the utilities – and manages the supply and demand balance. The PX ran the state-sponsored spot market in which the utilities – now called utility distribution companies (UDCs) – were required to buy all the requirements necessary to serve consumers who did not switch to another firm as well as to sell any energy they might produce. The obligation to purchase from CalPX was to be removed in 2002.

Current Industry Structure

Before reform, California's electricity supply industry was organised around three vertically integrated monopolies which owned and operated generation, transmission and distribution facilities. These companies, Pacific Gas and Electric (PG&E), San Diego Gas and Electric (SDG&E), and Southern California Edison (SCE), served all consumers in their exclusive franchise areas. The first two companies were also gas distribution companies. PG&E and SCE are about four times larger than SDG&E. There are also some large municipal utilities.

Federal legislation adopted in 1978 encouraged the development of independent power producers and allowed them to sell electricity to utilities, resulting in the creation of the Qualifying Facility (QF) program. California paid generously for QF-generated electricity and this encouraged sharp capacity additions within the state. By 1998 non-utility QF capacity accounted for nearly 20 per cent of the state's generating capacity. The share of non-utility capacity has increased since 1998, as California utilities had to divest major portions of their power capacity. By 2000, non-utility producers generated nearly half the electricity produced in California.

California's industry structure is currently in a state of flux. The state two largest utilities – PG&E and SCE – became insolvent in January 2001 and stopped paying their bills for power and other financial obligations. The former declared bankruptcy in April 2001.

Table 14

Major Generators in California

Company	Capacity (MW)	Market share (%)
Pacific Gas and Electric	7,387	24 %
Los Angeles Dept of Water and Power	4,915	16 %
AES Corporation	4,819	16 %
Reliant Energy	4,019	13 %
Southern California Edison	3,421	11 %
Duke Energy	2,764	9 %
San Diego Gas & Electric	1,216	4 %
Sacramento Municipal Utility District	828	3 %
Northern California Power Agency	645	2 %
FPL Energy	228	1 %
Others	490	2 %

Source: Sioshansi (2001).

The latter reached an agreement with the state in October 2001. The agreement provides that debts incurred during the crisis would be recovered over a two-year period from the difference between retail rates, which were increased in June 2001, and spot prices, which have subsided.

California's electricity supply depends heavily upon other states in the Western grid. Its interconnections allow for transfers of up to 17,926 MW. California habitually buys large quantities of energy from hydroelectric facilities in the Northwest and Southwest of the region during the spring and summer, whilst selling energy to the Northwest during off-peak periods in the winter.

Institutional Structure

The institutional structure of the United States is complex, with numerous actors at both the Federal and state level. Regulatory and legislative powers are divided between the states and the Federal government, with inter-state commerce being a Federal domain and intra-state commerce falling under state competence. Wholesale electricity sales and a large part of transmission services are within Federal competence while retail sales and distribution services are regulated by the states.

The main institutional players at Federal level are the Department of Energy (DOE), the Federal Energy Regulatory Commission (FERC), the Department of Justice (DOJ) and the Federal trade Commission (FTC). In addition, the California Public Utilities Commission and the California Energy Commission are involved in regulating the electricity industry.

The DOE is the ministry responsible for general energy policy and, specifically, for energy security, environmental quality and science and technology related to energy. The main regulatory institution at Federal level is FERC. Created in 1977 to replace the Federal Power Commission, the FERC regulates interstate commerce not only in electricity and hydroelectric power but also in natural gas and oil. In the electricity industry, FERC sets industry wide rules for sales and transmission in interstate commerce. It approves rates for private utilities, power marketers, power pools, power exchanges and independent system operators. It certifies small power producers and co-generation facilities and approves certain exemptions to the wholesale generator status. In addition, the FERC oversees mergers and acquisitions, reviews utility pooling and co-ordination agreements and monitors the industry. The antitrust agencies – the Department of Justice and the Federal Trade Commission – have jurisdictions that sometimes overlap with the FERC on electric utility mergers.

The California Public Utilities Commission regulates the rates and services of investor-owned electricity companies. Its jurisdiction covers distribution and retail sales. The Commission has a general mandate to supervise and regulate all utilities within California and to develop rules and other measures needed to implement reform. CPUC is specifically responsible for setting rates for electricity and distribution services, regulating service standards and monitoring utility operations for safety.

In California, by contrast with other states, the state government is responsible for siting and construction permits, which are issued by the Energy Commission[57]. This agency, established in 1974, is responsible, among other things, for monitoring power plant's compliance with environmental, safety and land-use standards.

Entry and Investment

Investment and System Development Process

The National Electric Reliability Council (NERC) oversees the reliability of the transmission network throughout the US and Canada. The Council includes several regional councils and ensures that there is a comparable and consistent plan for each region. The Western Systems Co-ordinating Council promotes electricity service reliability for the Western Interconnection. The Council: (i) develops criteria and policies for planning and operating reliability; (ii) oversees compliance through its Compliance and Monitoring Review Process and Reliability Management System; and (iii) facilitates transmission planning in the region. Seasonal assessment reports on reliability are published in both summer and winter, alongside long-term assessment reports for the next ten years.

The California Energy Commission has broad authority to decide whether the construction of a power plant is in California's best interest, regardless of local-government or public opposition. The Commission's mandate is complex. Its mission is defined as 'assessing, advocating for, and acting to improve energy systems that promote a strong economy and a healthy environment, while providing Californians with energy choices that are affordable, reliable, diverse, safe, and environmentally acceptable.'[58]

The Energy Commission delivers siting and construction permits for thermal power plants of 50 MW or larger. Plants smaller than 50 MW are licensed by city and council agencies. The siting

57. This body is composed of five appointed commissioners appointed by the governor to staggered five-year terms.

58. California Energy Commission (2001).

process varies according to the type of project proposed. For large and complex projects, developers must complete a 12-month Notice of Intention (NOI) process and apply for certification. The applicant has to propose at least three alternative sites. Such procedure is very demanding and time consuming, and it may deter applicants. The last NOI was filled in 1989 and withdraw in 1991. Previous to 1989, the last NOI dated from 1984.

All projects considered by the commission in recent years have been exempted from the NOI process. Applicants have to submit an application for certification. The Commission then has 12 months to make a decision. This period provides time for reviews and notifications to other agencies, if relevant, such as local air and water boards, the California Air Resources Board, the US Fish and Wildlife Service and the Federal Environmental Protection Agency.

Concerns have been raised about the Commission's ability to process applications in a timely manner. They have spiked up recently because of California's energy crisis. Although the entire review process is supposed to be completed in 12-months, the process has, in fact, averaged 17 months. This tardiness was due, in part, to external factors such as incomplete applications, delay by other federal, state, and local agencies and, in a few cases, public protests.

The energy crisis that began in the summer of 2000 and continued into 2001 forced a streamlining of procedures for siting review of new generation facilities. The Energy Commission expedited siting processes with the aim of providing new power capacity rapidly. Applications to build new power plants increased significantly. Between July 2000 and June 2001, nearly as many applications were submitted as in the three and a half years since deregulation was approved (18 applications against 19 in the previous period).

The commission developed a six-month certification process for thermal plants that are seen as having no adverse environmental impact. A four-month process was established for the expedited approval of simple-cycle facilities. A 21-day process now allows for the expedited approval of plants that will produce extra electricity to cover peak demand. The siting process for peaking plants has been widely used. Thirteen projects were approved by the Energy Commission by August 2001 — 11 of them peaker plants — with a total generating capacity of 9,024 MW. They were scheduled to go on-line between July 2001 and January 2004.

Main Constraints on Investment

Since the early 1980s California encouraged cogeneration and renewable energy. Utilities were required to buy power produced by certain Qualifying Facilities (QF) using renewable fuels under long-term contracts with very high prices[59]. Roughly 7,000 MW of QF generating capacity began operating by the early 1990s, bringing much excess capacity and high retail prices.

California has the most restrictive environmental requirements for power plants in the United States. This has limited plant development and raised investment costs. The state's air pollution standards are developed by the California Air Resources Board, which oversees the operation of its 35 local air-quality districts. Air quality control is ensured, in part, through pollution credits that are allocated to power plants every year, allowing them a certain level of emissions. The main pollutants covered by these permits are nitrogen oxides (NOx).

The rising cost of NOX permits has in turn, raised the cost of meeting environmental constraints. Moreover, environmental concerns have sparked strong opposition to construction of new plants. Supporting the environmentalists there have been special interests aiming to avoid construction near populated zones. These are the so-called NIMBY and BANANA syndromes. Nimby means 'Not In My Backyard' and BANANA stands for 'Build Absolutely Nothing Anywhere Near Anyone'.

Electricity restructuring gave rise to very contentious debates in California and other Western states during the second half of the

59. *Joskow (2001).*

1990s. The rules under which the industry would operate remained unclear. Uncertainty about the new rules of the game is clearly one reason why no new generating capacity was added in California and other Western states. In California, the investor-owned utilities submitted only one application for a new power plant from 1991 to 1995.

Complex institutional structures and decision-making processes forestalled efforts to avoid power blackouts and to head off the subsequent crisis. Despite forecasts of potential power shortages in 1999, the California Independent System Operator did not initiate any program to secure peaking capacity.

California's crisis was acknowledged by the federal government only in mid-December 2000. Within the state, initiatives to speed up the siting review process or otherwise encourage completion of new generation plants came only in 2001. Furthermore, relations between FERC, the CPUC and the ISO became more difficult as the crisis intensified. The FERC put pressure on the California parties to implement reforms that it felt to be appropriate regardless of the views of the other authorities.

■ Market Design

In 1998, California opened the market to retail competition and set up a spot market. The California Power Exchange (CalPX) was set up as a voluntary pool, although the major utilities in California were obliged to sell and buy only through the pool for the first four years of operation until March 31, 2002. CalPX conducted daily auctions to allow trading of electricity both in the forward day-ahead market and in the hour-ahead market.

In the day-ahead market, the PX accepted demand and generation bids from which it calculated the Market Clearing Price (MCP), and submitted balanced demand and supply schedules to the system operator. The clearing price was determined for each hour of the scheduling day. The System Operator then determined whether the dispatch plan proposed by the PX would result in congestion and then submitted an adjusted schedule to the PX. Finally, the PX would determine clearing prices in each zone and the final dispatch schedule. CalPX also ran markets for ancillary services, real-time balancing and congestion management. In the hour-ahead market, bids were submitted to the PX at least 2 hours before the hour of operation. The MCP was determined the same way as in the day-ahead market.

Non competitive bidding contributed to high wholesale energy prices. Under-scheduling of the demand and supply of power seems to have been used to raise prices. This device frequently pushed the ISO to operate in a crisis mode to secure enough electricity to avoid blackouts. The requirement that the utilities rely entirely on the PX to buy and sell power allowed both buyers and sellers to manipulate the market.

Joskow (2001) points out that prices before the 'crisis' – from April 1998 to April 2000 – roughly reflected expectations at the time restructuring began. Indeed, wholesales prices were forecast to start at an hourly average of about \$25/MWh and rise to about \$30/MWh as excess capacity was gradually dissipated. Ancillary services prices were expected to represent about 2 per cent of the cost of generation services rather than the 10-15 per cent that it represented in practice.

High prices were accompanied by very high price volatility in the summer of 2000, and this trend continued into early 2001. The power crisis forced reform of market rules and closure of the California Power Exchange. In January 2001, the state adopted emergency measures to control prices charged by generation facilities owned by the state's utilities to buy additional power through a state agency. The state also began to experience rolling blackouts because of regional power shortages.

Prices were limited by price caps that decreased from \$1,000/MWh in 1998 down to \$750 in 1999 and \$250 in 2000. These caps were not binding on surrounding states, and this created incentives for generating firms to sell outside of California whenever outside prices were higher than the price cap.

The FERC voted on April 26, 2001 to establish a benchmark price for wholesale electricity sold in California in emergency situations. The benchmark is the cost of power from the highest-cost generating unit in service. All generators bidding at or below the benchmark price are to receive that price. Generators exceeding the benchmark will have to justify their prices or be obliged to pay refunds. On 18 June 2001 the benchmark system was extended to all hours of the day and to the entire West of the US. Since the benchmark equals the cost of generation from the highest-priced unit, there should still be a strong incentive to provide new supplies. Requirement of justification of prices above the benchmark also reduces the risk of market manipulation.

Programs were set up to curb demand during peak demand periods including incentive programs to reduce peak demand, an education campaign on energy conservation, calls for voluntary efforts to reduce electricity consumption, energy efficiency improvements and rebates on reduced consumption[60].

Retail rates for the customers of PG&E and SCE have risen sharply. The 10% reduction from 1998 rates which was embodied in the original transition scheme was roughly cancelled out by a 1 cent per kWh rate increase on 4 January 2001. An additional increase of 3 cents per kWh was imposed on March 27, effective June 1. Small customers representing 60% of residential demand have been legally exempted from additional increases. The average rate hike for other customers is 4.5 cents, or about 46%.

The situation in California's electricity market stabilised from the third quarter of 2001 (the last rolling blackout was recorded on

60. *2001 Summer Conservation Report, California Energy Commission.*

8 May 2001) with reliability being restored, wholesale prices returning to normal levels and investment activity peaking up. To address the financial crisis of the utilities, the state of California has been buying power on behalf of the utilities both in the spot market and through long term contracts. Power purchases are estimated at US$ 12.45 billion and 68 683 000 MWh for the period January 2001-February 2002. In February 2002 the California regulator agreed to a rate increase to finance the approximately US$ 10 billion in debt incurred by the government of California (through the Water Resources Department) to purchase power. This form of power procurement is only intended as an interim solution and consideration is being given to new market arrangements. However, the future regulation of the industry remains uncertain.

In August 2001 the California Consumer Power and Conservation Financing Authority (CPA) was established with a general mandate to serve as a vehicle in acquiring power to meet energy needs in California and securing a sufficient reserve of power. CPA is authorised to issue up to US$ 5 billion in revenue bonds to finance energy projects and conservation programs. CPA will focus on financing the deployment of renewable and distributed generation and is also considering load management and conservation projects.

Performance

Investment in new generating capacity has failed to keep pace with demand growth in California over the last six years and reserves have been eroding. The deterioration in generating capacity reserves started well before market reforms were implemented, and continued afterwards. Investment failed to materialise in the first place because electricity demand was not expected to grow significantly in California after the severe recession in the early 1990s. But the state's economy boomed from 1995 to 2000 and electricity demand grew quickly. Demand growth in neighbouring states was also high, reducing the amount of power available for export to California. In 2000, a hot summer followed by an unusually cold winter boosted demand well above forecasts throughout the West.

Capacity utilisation has remained relatively high in California over the last ten years, usually 50 per cent or more. It increased in California after 1998. In 2000 capacity utilisation approached 60 per cent.

Reserve margins fluctuated over the last decade, substantially decreasing from 20 per cent in 1995 to 6 per cent in 1999 and less than 10 per cent in 2000. California's peak demand increased by more than 5,500 MW in the three years from 1997, while generating capacity increased by less than 700 MW over the same period. As a result there were rotating blackouts during about 260 hours over the summer of 2000.

The generation fuel mix is well diversified among gas, hydro and other renewables, coal and nuclear fuels. Gas accounted for nearly 40 per cent of the fuels used to generate electricity in 2000, compared to 30 per cent in 1990. The predominance of gas-fired generation has rendered generators very sensitive to gas price changes, such as the steep price rise in 2000.

The California Power Exchange (CalPX) worked fairly well for a year and a half. From the summer of 2000, however, electricity prices in southern California rose dramatically to all-time highs. The price of wholesale electricity sold on CalPX started escalating around June 2000[61]. Wholesale prices increased by 500 per cent between the second half of 1999 and the second half of 2000. By December 2000, prices on the CalPX stood at an average of $376.99 per MWh, about twelve times the average clearing price of $29.71 in December 1999.

---

61. Joskow (2001).

Figure 35

Capacity and Demand in California, 1990-2000

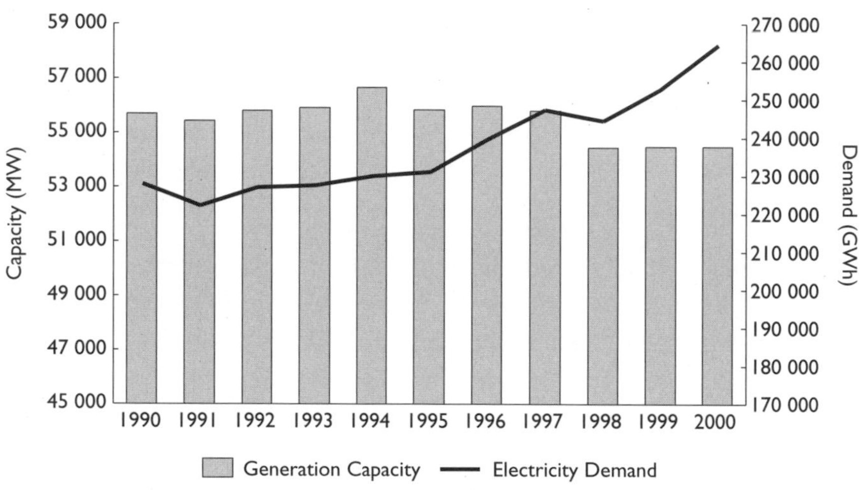

Source: Data from the California Energy Commission and the Energy Information Administration.
Note: Capacity encompasses utility and nonutility capacity. Year 2000 estimated.

Figure 36

Capacity Utilisation in California, 1990-2000

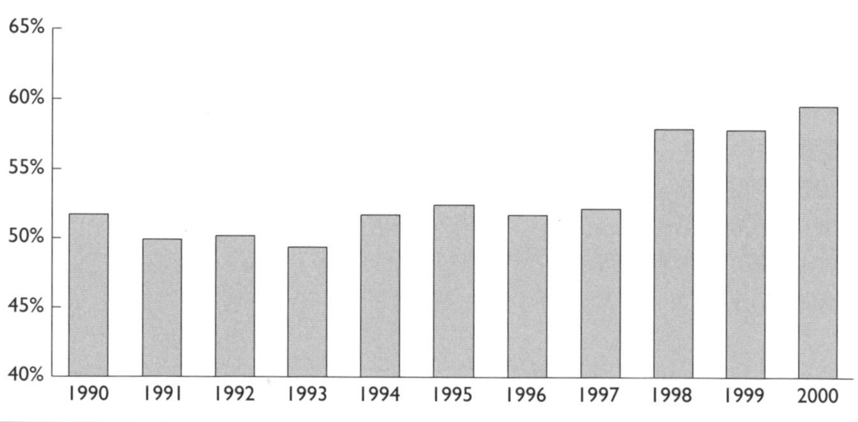

Source: Data from the California Energy Commission and the Energy Information Administration.

Figure 37

Reserve Margin and Demand Growth in California, 1990-2000

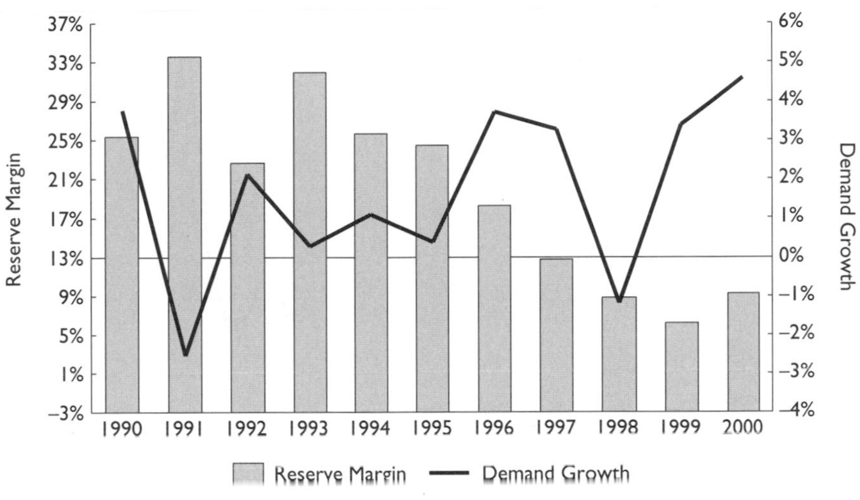

Source: Data from the California Energy Commission and the US Energy Information Administration.

Figure 38

Fuel Mix in California, 1990-2000

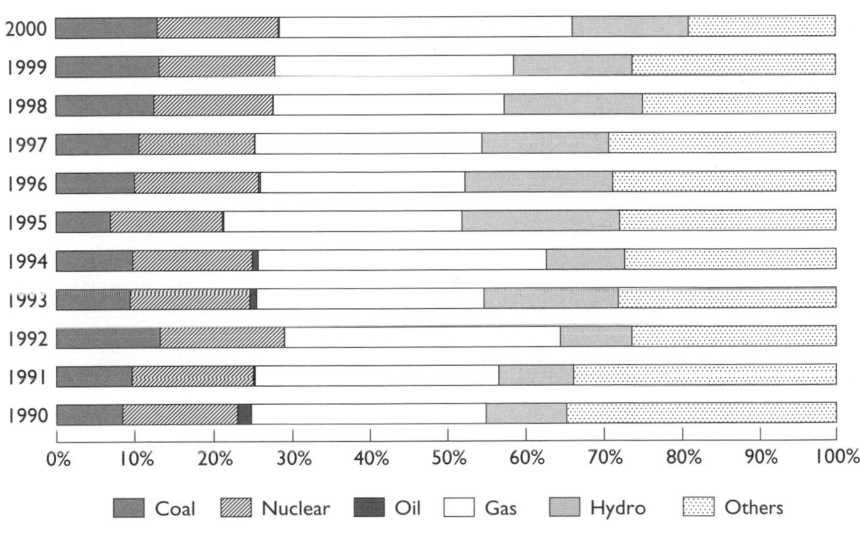

Source: Data from the California Energy Commission.

Figure 39

California PX Day-ahead and ISO Prices

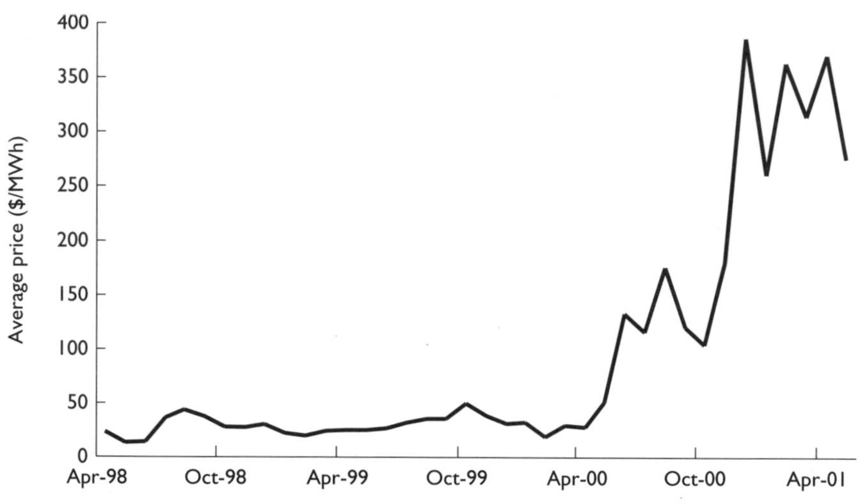

Source: Data from Joskow (2001).

Note: Prices are from Californian ISO from February 2001, as the PX was then closed.

Figure 40

Retail Prices in California, 1990-2000

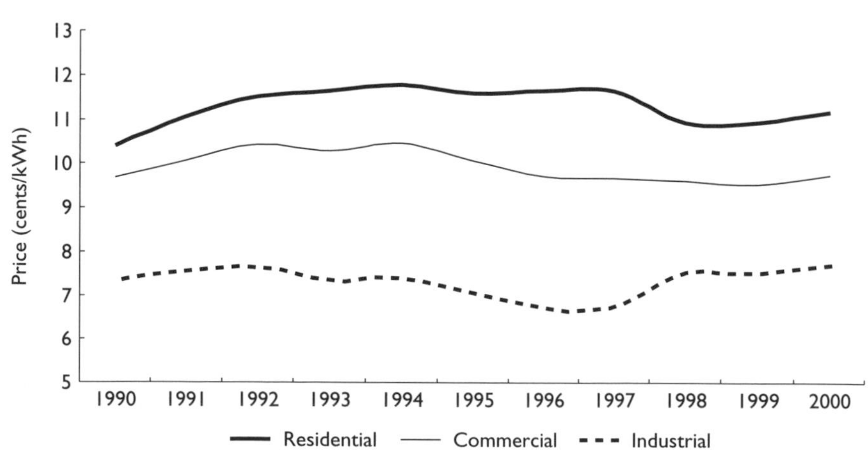

Source: Data from the California Energy Commission.

By contrast, retail prices were mostly fixed until early 2001. The exception was SDG&E, which was freed of the retail price freeze in January 2000. Since prices were allowed to adjust to changes in wholesale prices, a steep increase in retail electricity prices occurred in southern California in the summer of 2000. By July 2000, residential electricity rates for SDG&E had increased to approximately 16 cents per kWh, up from about 11 cents per kWh at the same period of the previous year. To halt the increase in retail prices, they were capped once again. California's legislature established a ceiling of 6.5 cents per kWh on the energy component of electricity bills for residential, small commercial and lighting customers of SDG&E. Retail prices remained deregulated only for the company's large commercial and industrial consumers. The retail prize freeze remained in place for the two largest California utilities, PG&E and SCE. There, the high wholesale prices had a disastrous impact: PG&E and SCE became insolvent.

Assessment

California's electricity crisis had two components. On the physical side, there was insufficient capacity to meet demand. On the financial side, a number of circumstances combined to put the industry in an unsustainable situation. This study is primarily concerned with the physical dimension of the crisis.

The investment shortage happened despite the fact that prices were relatively high compared to the cost of building new capacity. A number of institutional and regulatory elements contributed to the inadequacy of investment:

- An extremely cumbersome and slow authorisation system for new generation plants, subject to frequent challenges from various groups and similar problems affecting the construction of transmission lines;
- An institutional set up that failed to identify the coming crisis; in particular, neither the system operator nor the state regulatory institutions anticipated a capacity shortfall;

- High regulatory risk as preparation for reform dragged on over several years.

While it is hard to assess the weight of each factor in provoking the crisis, the inadequate authorisation system played an important role. New investment took place when legal and regulatory barriers were eased. A number of measures have been implemented to facilitate this process and ensure that planned investments materialise. These include reducing the various hurdles that delay the approval of investment projects and providing incentives for investment in generation and transmission capacity. Investment is now flowing into California's market. Planned capacity additions over the 2000-2005 period are large. The California ISO 2001 Summer Assessment reports that some 54 generation projects with 30 gigawatts of capacity are forecast to enter into service between 2002 and 2005.

The financial crisis suffered by California's utilities can be traced back to some inadequate arrangements adopted for the transition to a liberalised market. These included limits to risk hedging through long-term contracts, a mandatory pool that prevented other forms of risk hedging and fixed retail tariffs that failed to reflect fluctuations in wholesale prices. High gas prices and the rising price of NOx permits combined with high demand to expose the weaknesses of such arrangements. Market power and market manipulation have also contributed to some extent.

The California experience provides important lessons to reformers including the need to remain vigilant about the institutional and legal framework in which electricity markets operate. Legal and regulatory barriers played a major role in producing an investment crisis. The lack of awareness of its imminence and the late reaction to it underline the need for governments to monitor reliability and investment developments during the transition to a liberalised electricity market.

Pennsylvania-New Jersey-Maryland (PJM)

The PJM Interconnection is a multi-state market on the East Coast of the United States comprising all or part of six jurisdictions — Pennsylvania, New Jersey, Maryland, Delaware, Virginia and the District of Columbia. The market is run by member utilities under the authority of an independent governing board which has ultimate decision-making authority. The board co-exists with a committee of stakeholders which makes most decisions. Decision-making structure is complex as illustrated by the voting process. There are four groups of stakeholders and each one is polled separately; an average two-thirds majority among the four groups is required. PJM activities include both running a power exchange and the operation of the system. PJM already existed as a power pool in the pre-competition era.

■ Structure of the Industry

Industry Reform

Each state in the PJM system is implementing its own regulatory arrangements for retail markets. Most have adopted a gradual approach to restructuring and retail competition. Pennsylvania was the first state to reform and a fully opened retail market is fully operational. In December 1996, the state legislature authorised choice for electricity customers in Pennsylvania to be phased in from 1999 to the end of the year 2001. Maryland's Electric Consumer Choice and Competition Act went into effect in July 1999 and New Jersey started reform in August 1999, providing retail electricity choice to all consumers in July 2000. Pennsylvania is one of the most active retail electricity markets in the United States, with customer switching rates well above those in other states.

Current Industry Structure

The market is fairly unconcentrated at the regional level, with the biggest firm's market share at less than 20 per cent. Six firms own nearly 75 per cent of the market's generating capacity. The major utilities in the PJM area are Public Service Electric & Gas Company (New Jersey), PECO Energy Company (Pennsylvania), Pennsylvania Power & Light Company (Pennsylvania), Potomac Electric Power Company (Maryland), Pennsylvania Electric Company (Pennsylvania), and Baltimore Gas & Electric Company (Maryland).

Table 15

Major Generating Companies in PJM

	Capacity (MW)	Market share (%)
PSEG	12,184	19%
EXELON	10,367	16%
PPL	8,638	13%
Constellation	7,010	11%
Mirant	5,545	9%
Reliant	4,427	7%
Others	15,855	25%

Source: Elaborated from RDI Power Database.

Institutional Structure

The institutional structure in the states covered by PJM is similar to the one in California, but slightly more complex. At the Federal level, the actors in both jurisdictions are the same. At the state level, the main actors are the state public utilities commissions: the Delaware Commission, the Public Utility Commission of Pennsylvania, the New Jersey Board of Public Utilities, and the Maryland Public Services Commission. The responsibilities of these commissions are similar to those of the California PUC. They have a general mandate to supervise and regulate all utilities within their state. They regulate distribution activities and retail sales of investor-owned electricity companies. By contrast with California, the Mid-Atlantic states are directly responsible for the siting and construction permits needed to build new power plants.

■ Entry and Investment

Investment and System Development Process

Responsibility for the reliability of power supply is shared by several institutions. At the federal level, NERC oversees the reliability of bulk power markets and issues a specific plan for each region. The Mid-Atlantic Area Council (MAAC) is the regional council for the PJM Interconnection. MAAC: (i) develops criteria for planning and operating reliability; (ii) oversees compliance with these criteria; and (iii) promotes a regional transmission planning process.

Regional assessments are performed semi-annually for the near term and annually for the coming decade. In its larger-term assessment, MAAC evaluates future power needs and the electricity generating capacity needed to meet them. In its forecasts, MAAC takes as input PJM plans for expansion of transmission capacity, and takes into account generation projects which have been authorised. Actual construction and operation of authorised plants is, however, questionable.

There is a pool-wide planning process for the PJM control area to ensure that adequate generating capacity will become available in a timely manner. Each year, a calculation is made of the reserve levels necessary to maintain a loss-of-load probability of one day in ten years and a reserve requirement is set for two years in the future. This two-year period is supposed to allow for site preparation, fuel supply procurement and construction of required capacity.

PJM calculates the amount of generating capacity required to meet the reliability criteria and sets capacity obligations. PJM requires those of its members that are Load Serving Entities to maintain a minimum reserve capacity over expected peak load through Installed Capacity requirements. The margin required by PJM is around 20 per cent of anticipated peak demand. Installed capacity obligations can be traded over the Capacity Credit Market (CCM).

Licensing procedures for new power generating plants lie with state regulators and consist mostly of environmental permitting requirements. The review process requires an applicant to prove : (i) technical and managerial competence; (ii) compliance with applicable environmental laws and regulation; and (iii) financial integrity and qualification to do business in the state. The review process is short. In New Jersey, for instance, the standard time for review is 60 days after receipt of the application — compared to 12 months in California. If the standard time is not sufficient to reach a final conclusion, the New Jersey Board of Public Utilities may issue a provisional licence.

Main Constraints on Investment

In PJM, there are no major barriers to entry into power generation. Licensing procedures within PJM states are expeditious and do not impose particular constraints. Capacity additions in PJM have been steady and the trend continuous. Between 1999 and 2000, 702 MW of new generating capacity came on-line in PJM. Requests to interconnect according to MAAC's Reliability Assessment for 2000-09 amount to more than 38,000 MW of generation capacity.

Concerns have arisen regarding the possible effects of an Environmental Protection Agency regulation that requires abatement of NOx in all states within PJM by 2003. This is, however, a limited concern given the relatively low share of gas-fired capacity within the region.

■ Market Design

PJM gradually developed markets for energy, generating capacity and transmission capacity. Market-based energy pricing was introduced in April 1999 with a market clearing price based on competitive bids; previously dispatch was based on costs.

Participants in the wholesale market trade in two ways. Firm sales may take the form of bilateral contracts. All other power is traded through a centralised spot market. PJM has no markets for ancillary services.

PJM operates a day-ahead market in which generators submit offers on an hourly basis and dispatch is determined on the basis of these offers. Only one price bid per day can be submitted by any one bidder. These prices are computed for the actual dispatch every five minutes.

Since 1999, PJM has limited congestion by setting nodal prices for energy, known as locational marginal prices (LMP). The PJM dispatch software takes account of all transmission constraints and, if necessary, calculates a separate marginal price at each of around 2000 grid-access points[62]. Prices are determined after dispatch so that they take account of real-time events.

There is a bid cap in the PJM energy market[63] of $ 1,000/MWh. In the summer of 2000, this bid cap was extended to other states, as differing price caps were providing incentives to generators to neglect their reliability requirements. This happened because bids into the PJM market were not firm. Under pressure from the FERC, the PJM agreed to introduce a two-stage market in 2000. Accepted day-ahead bids become firm and a separate hour-ahead market is used to balance the system.

---

62. Complexity and impediments to trading have been partly overcome by averaging LMP prices into a small number of zones and making other changes to simplify the system.

63. States in PJM impose retail price caps. However, generation 'shopping credits' were set high enough to reduce exposure to price volatility through long-term contracts. Over 780,000 retail customers have switched to new generation suppliers.

PJM also operates an Installed Capacity (ICAP) market. All load-serving entities (LSEs) are required to purchase ICAP in addition to energy, or else they must pay a penalty to the system operator which is then redistributed among the generators. The capacity deficiency rate is set to $177.30/MW-day. This requirement aims to ensure that electricity retailers have reserved sufficient generating capacity to meet their consumers' demand. The reserve margin which LSEs are required to maintain is a function of the annual peak load served by each entity.

LSEs may fulfil the required capacity obligation by owning plants and/or by buying capacity rights from other generators. This system is intended to prevent shortages; yet it has no bearing on who actually generates power. To facilitate ICAP trading, PJM has run a day-ahead capacity market since January 1999. In mid-1999 it was broadened to include monthly and multi-monthly markets. There is a mandatory aspect to the capacity market as generators with unsold ICAP are obliged to offer it in the day-ahead market.

■ Performance

Demand growth throughout PJM and in surrounding power pools has been moderate. Over 6,000 MW of generation capacity was added to PJM over the past decade, which was more than sufficient to cover demand. Surrounding regions followed the same trend. A further 6,000 MW are currently planned or under construction in the PJM control area.

Capacity utilisation has consistently been high in Pennsylvania in the last decade, usually over 50 per cent. Capacity utilisation increased after reform, reaching 55 per cent.

The reserve margin has been fluctuating in PJM over the last five years, at around 15 per cent. This reflects the framework that PJM

Figure 41

Capacity Utilisation in Pennsylvania, 1990-2000

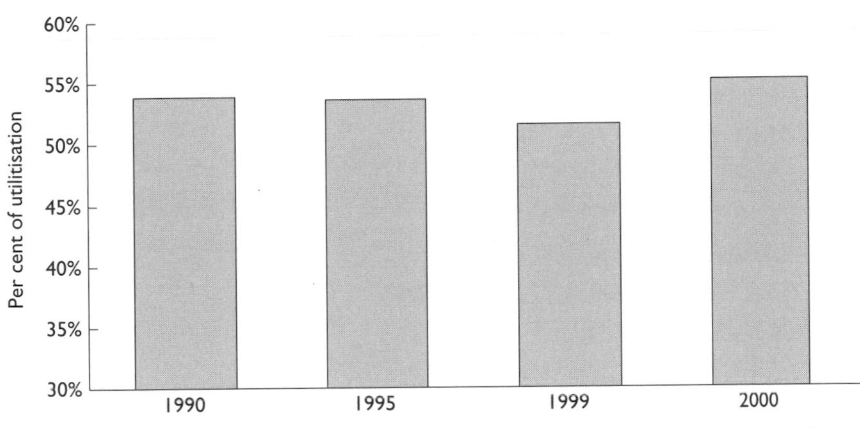

Source: Data from the US Energy Information Administration.

Figure 42

Reserve Margins and Capacity in PJM, 1995-2000

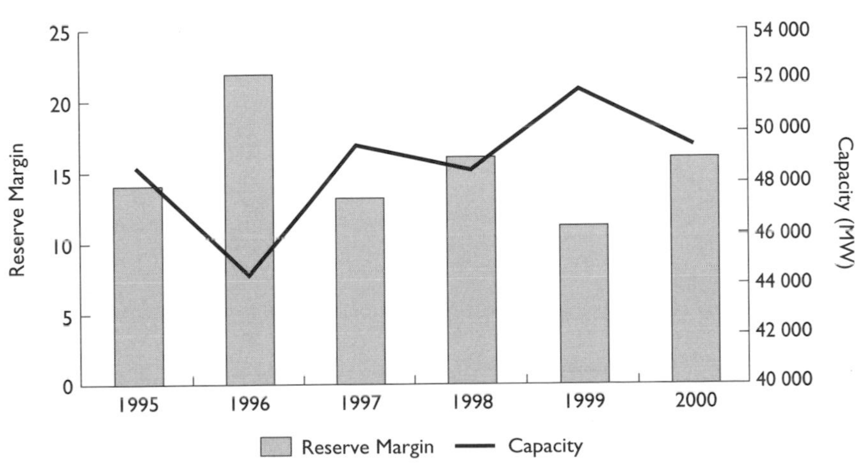

Source: PJM Annual Report on Operations.

Figure 43

Fuel Mix in Pennsylvania, 1990-2000

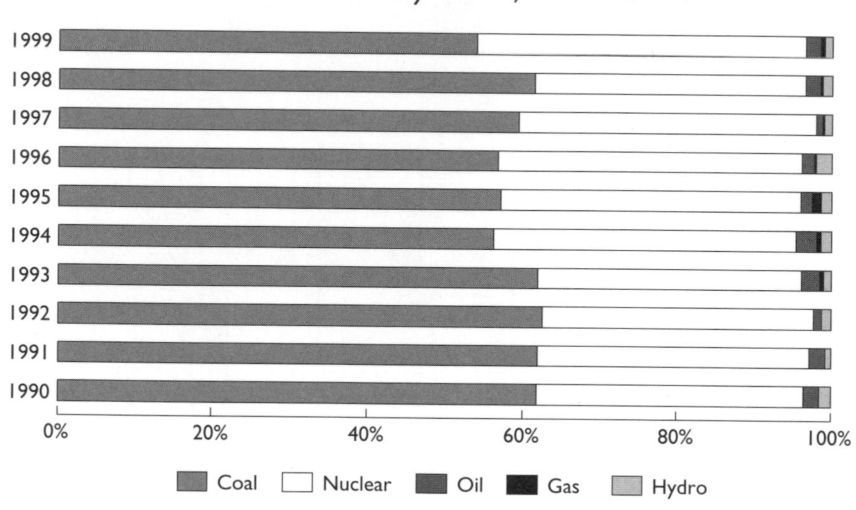

Source: Data from the Pennsylvania PUC Electric Utility Operational Report.

Figure 44

Wholesale Price in PJM and Volatility, 1998-2000

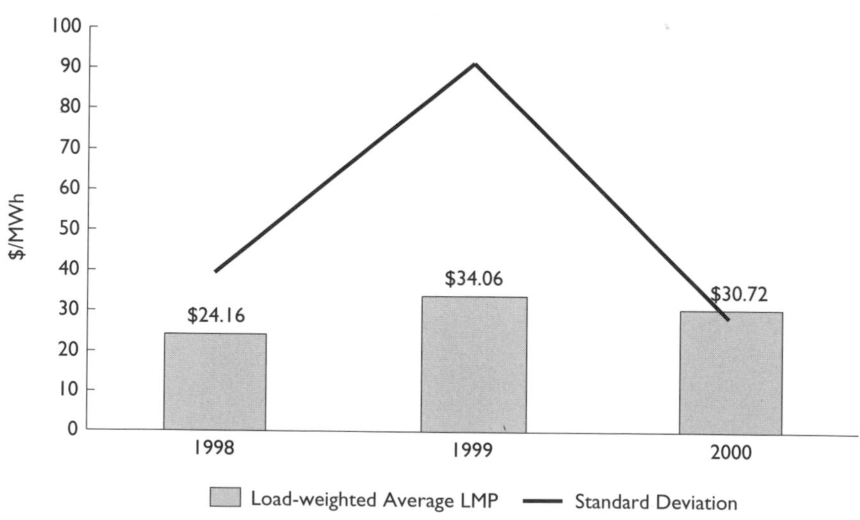

Source: PJM Market Monitoring Unit (2001).

uses to ensure that enough generating reserve be available to satisfy demand. PJM's 20 per cent reserve margin requirement is applied to firm load only. Interruptible load accounts for an additional 4 to 5 per cent of PJM's total load.

More than 60 per cent of the power generated in PJM is from fossil fuels (31 per cent from coal, 11 per cent from oil) and nuclear (22 per cent from nuclear plants in 2000). At the end of the year 2000, gas represented only 4 per cent of the fuel mix in the region. More than half the energy consumed in the PJM region is produced in Pennsylvania. The state's fuel mix is dominated by coal and nuclear, which total more than 95 per cent of generation.

Wholesale energy prices in PJM rose in 1999 following the introduction of competitive bidding reaching $34/MWh, about $10 more than the previous year. Prices also became more volatile, and there were some large price spikes in July 1999. Prices decreased in 2000 to $31/MWh. Prices remained below $100/MWh most of the time (98 per cent of the hours), and volatility has fallen below pre-competitive levels.

ICAP prices have increased greatly since 1999, especially in the day-ahead credit market. The mean price for ICAP traded daily nearly quadrupled between 1999 and 2000. The cost of a megawatt of capacity amounted was $1,304 in 2000. In the monthly market, ICAP prices have also risen. The PJM Market Monitoring Unit has recommended some changes in market rules to modify incentives in the capacity market, to require all LSEs to serve load on a longer-term basis and to require capacity resources to be offered on a comparable long-term basis. Overall, PJM considers that the energy and capacity markets were reasonably competitive in 1999 and 2000 but points out that there are potential threats to competition in these markets that require ongoing scrutiny and may, in some cases, require action in order to maintain competition.

Figure 45

Retail Prices in Pennsylvania, 1990-2000

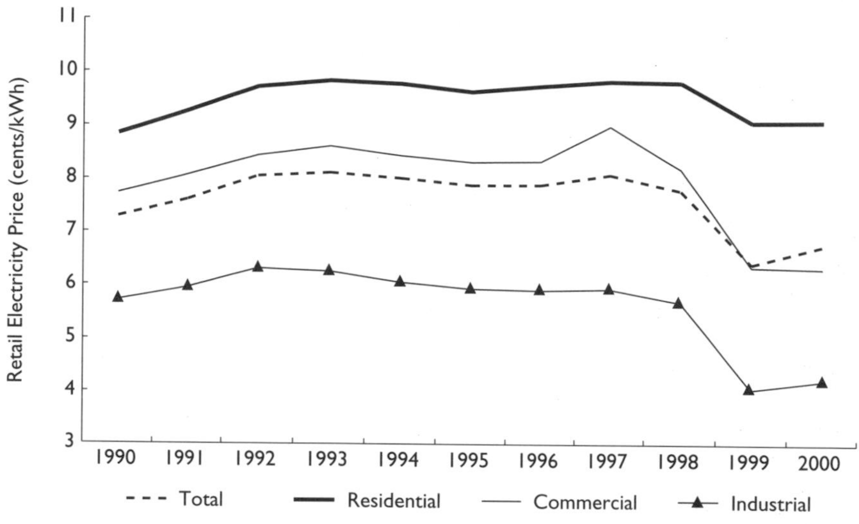

Source: Data from the Pennsylvania PUC Electric Utility Operational Report.

Table 16

Installed Capacity traded in the PJM Capacity Credit Market ($/MW)

	Daily ICAP	Monthly ICAP	Multi-monthly ICAP
1999	374	241	740
2000	1,304	634	927

Source: PJM Market Monitoring Unit (2001).

Assessment

In PJM, reserve margins have remained stable over the last five years, and security of supply is perceived to be assured. Generation capacity has grown steadily and is adequate to meet demand. Surrounding regions have followed the same trend.

Capacity utilisation has been consistently high. The market is, however, very new and the evidence is consequently limited.

High wholesale prices relative to entry cost help to explain PJM's good investment performance. Reliability is monitored very closely by several institutions, which rely on collaboration between the regional reliability council and the system operator.

There are no significant entry barriers for the construction of new generating plants in PJM. The siting review process is expeditious. Regulatory risk has been low, as electricity market reform did not fundamentally change market institutions and operational rules.

The installed capacity market operated by PJM is working aptly, although it is too new to make any firm assessment. The combination of an ICAP market with a bid cap has diminished market volatility, which rose severely after competitive bidding was first introduced into the energy market. There are some fears, however, that the price levels for capacity are too high, given existing capacity levels. Other issues concerning ICAP markets are being reviewed by PJM, notably those of generators' time horizon and of the penalty levels to be paid by LSEs which fail to meet their capacity requirements. Market experience has revealed that there may be unexpected interactions between market prices for different products, and also between regional markets with different rules.

REFERENCES

Acutt, M., Eliott, C. and Robinson, T. (2001) 'Credible Regulatory Threat', *Energy Policy* 29, pp. 911-16.

Armstrong, M., Cowan, S. and Vickers, J. (1994) *Regulatory Reform - Economic Analysis and British Experience*, Oxford University Press: Oxford.

Asthana et al. "Finding the Balance of Power". The McKinsey Quarterly, 2001 number 4.

Australian Energy News (2000) 'The VoLL Debate – Putting a Price on Power System Reliability', September, p. 26.

Bar-Ilan, A. And Strange, W. C. (1996) 'Investment Lags', *The American Economic Review*, Volume 86, Issue 3, pp. 610-22.

Bernanke, B. S. (1983) 'Irreversibility, Uncertainty, and Cyclical Investment', *The Quarterly Journal of Economics*, pp. 85-106.

Birnbaum, L., Grobbel, C., Ninios, P., Röthel, T. and Volpin, A. (2000) 'A Shopper's Guide to Electricity Assets in Europe', The McKinsey Quarterly, No. 2.

Borenstein, S. (2001) 'The Trouble with Electricity Markets (and Some Solutions)', *POWER Working Paper*, PWP-081, University of California Energy Institute, Berkeley.

Borenstein, S., Bushnell, J. and Wolak, F. (2000) *Diagnosing Market Power in California's Restructured Wholesale Electricity Market*, Mimeo.

Bowring, J. E. and Gramlich, R. E. (2000) 'The Role of Capacity Obligations in a Restructured Pennsylvania-New Jersey-Maryland Electricity Market', *Electricity Journal*, November, pp. 57-67.

Bunn, D.W., Day, C, and Vlahos, K. (1998) 'Understanding Latent Market Power in the Electricity Pool of England & Wales', in *Pricing Energy in a Competitive Market*, Electric Power Research Institute, 3412 Hillview Ave, Palo Alto, CA 94304 USA.

Energy Information Administration (1995) *Performance Issues for a Changing Electric Power Industry*. US Department of Energy.

Fehr, N.Von der and D. Harbord (1997*c*) 'Competition in Electricity Spot Markets. Economic Theory and International Experience', Mimeo, Department of Economics, University of Oslo.

Fehr, N.H. von der and D. Harbord (1997*a*) *Capacity investment and dynamic efficiency in market-based electricity industries*, mimeo, Department of Economics, University of Oslo.

Fehr, N.H. von der and D. Harbord (1997*b*) *Oligopoly, capacity competition and uncertainty under different regulatory regimes*, Mimeo, Department of Economics, University of Oslo.

Fehr, N.H. von der, and D. Harbord (1995) 'Capacity investments and long-run efficiency in market-based electricity industries', in *Competition in the Electricity Supply Industry – Experience from Europe and the United States*, O.J. Olsen (ed.), Copenhagen.

Financial Times Energy (2001) Power UK, Issue 87, May.

Fisher, J.V. and Duane, T. P. (2001) 'Trends in Electricity consumption, Peak Demand, and Generating Capacity in California and the Western Grid 1977-2000', *Power Working Paper*, PWP-085, University of California energy Institute, Berkeley.

Ford, A. (2000) 'Boom and Bust? Understanding the Power Plant Construction Cycle', *Public Utilities Fortnightly*, 15th July, pp. 36-45.

Ford, A. (1999) 'Cycles in Competitive Electricity Markets: A Simulation Study of the Western United States', *Energy Policy*, Volume 29, pp. 637-58.

Gray, P., Helm, D. R. and Powell, A. (1996) 'Competition vs. Regulation in British Electricity Generation', in McKerron, G. and Pearson, P. (Eds.), *The British Energy Experience: A Lesson or a Warning?*, London.

Green, R. (1996) 'Increasing Competition in the British Electricity Spot Market', *The Journal of Industrial Economics*, Vol. XLIV, No.2, pp 205-216.

Green, R. J., and Newbery, D. M. (1998) Comments on Review of Energy Sources for Power Generation: Consultation Document, Mimeo, Cambridge.

Green, R.J. (1999) 'The Electricity Contract Market in England & Wales' *Journal of Industrial Economics*, Vol. XLVII, No 1, pp.107-124.

Green, R.J (1998) 'England & Wales: A competitive electricity market?' *Power Working Paper* PWP-060, University of California Energy Institute.

Haas, R. and Auer, H. (2001) *The Relevance of Excess Capacities for Competition in European Electricity Markets*, Mimeo.

Harvey, S. M. and Hogan, W. W. (2001) *On the Exercise of Market Power through Strategic Withholding in California*, Mimeo.

Henney, A. (2000) *The practices and Principles of Transmission Pricing*, Mimeo.

Herguera, I. (2000) 'Bilateral Contracts and the Spot Market for Electricity: Some Observations on the British and the NordPool Experiences', *Utilities Policy*, Volume 9, pp. 73-80.

Hobbs, B. F., Íñon, J. and Stoft, S. E. (2001) 'Installed Capacity Requirements and Price Caps: Oil on the Water, or Fuel on the Fire?' *The Electricity Journal*, July, pp. 23-34.

Hunt, S. and G. Shuttleworth (1996) *Competition and Choice in Electricity*, J. Wiley & Sons Ltd, West Sussex.

Joskow, P. L. (2001) *California's Electricity Crisis*, Mimeo.

Joskow, P. L. and Khan, E. (2001) *A Quantitative Analysis of Pricing Behaviour in California's Electricity Market during Summer 2000*, Mimeo.

Joskow, P. (1997) 'Restructuring, Competition and Regulatory Reform in the US Electricity Sector', *Journal of Economic Perspectives*, Vol. 11, No. 3, pp. 119-138.

Kirsch, L. D. and Rajaraman, R. (2001) 'Assuring Enough Generation: Whose Job and How to Do It?', *Public Utilities Fortnightly*, 15th April, pp. 34-42.

Levesque, C. J. (2000) 'Merchant Mania: Regional Markets Draw Gen Plant Projects', *Public Utilities Fortnightly*, 1st January, pp. 26-30.

Mansur, E. T. (2001) 'Pricing Behaviour in the Initial Summer of the Restructured PJM Wholesale Electricity Market', *Power Working Paper* PWP-083, University of California Energy Institute.

Newbery, D.M. (1997) 'Pool Reform and Competition in Electricity', *DAE Working Paper* 9734, Cambridge.

Newbery, D.M. (2002) 'Problems of Liberalising the Electricity Industry', *European Economic Review*. In Press

Oxford Economics Research Associates (2001) 'The Value of Flexibility', *The Utilities Journal*, January, pp. 16-7.

Puller, S. L. (2001) 'Pricing and Firm Conduct in California's Deregulated Electricity Market', *Power Working Paper*, PWP-080, University of California Energy Institute, Berkeley.

Seiple, C. D. (2000) 'Bust on the Horizon? Are Developers Building More Power Generation Capacity than U.S. Markets Can Bear?', *Public Utilities Fortnightly*, 15th January, pp. 8-9.

Sheffrin, A. (2001) *Empirical Evidence of Strategic Bidding in California ISO Real Time Market*, California ISO.

Sioshansi, F. P. (2001) 'California's dysfunctional electricity market: policy lessons on market restructuring, *Energy Policy* 29 (9), pp. 735-742.

Stoft, S. (2001) *Power System Economics*, forthcoming (abstract available on www.stoft.com).

Stoft, S. (2000) 'PJM's Capacity Market in a Price-Spike World', *POWER Working Paper* PWP-077, University of California Energy Institute.

Vazquez, C., M. Rivier, and JI Perez Arriaga (2001) A market approach to long-term security of supply, IIT Working Paper 0078, March, 2001. IIT Madrid.

Wilson, J. F. (2000) 'Scarcity, Market Power, and Price Caps in Wholesale Electric Power Markets', *The Electricity Journal*, pp. 33-46.

STATISTICAL AND LEGAL REFERENCES

Competition Commission (2001) *AES and British Energy: A Report on References Made under Section 12 of the Electricity Act 1989*, Presented to the DGES in December 2000, London: CC.

Commission for Electricity Regulation (2001) Proposed Decision under Regulation 3(4) of SI No. 49 Electricity Regulation Act (Trading Arrangements in Electricity), CER/01/40, Dublin.

Department of Trade and Industry (1997) Review of Energy Sources for Power Stations: Terms of Reference, HMSO, London, UK.

Department of Trade and Industry (1998) Conclusions of the Review of Energy Sources for Power Generation and Government Response to Fourth and Fifth Reports of the Trade and Industry Committee, London: Stationary Office.

Department of Trade and Industry (1998a) A Fair Deal for Consumers: Modernising the Framework for Utility Regulation, CM 3898, HMSO, London, UK.

Department of Trade and Industry (1998b) Review of Energy Sources for Power Stations Interim Conclusions, HMSO, London, UK.

Department of Trade and Industry (2000) *UK Energy Sector Indicators*, London: Stationary Office.

Department of Trade and Industry (2001) *Guidance on Background Information to Accompany Notifications under Section 14(1) of the Energy Act 1976 and Applications under Section 36 of the Electricity Act 1989*, London: Stationary Office.

Department of Trade and Industry (2001) *Digest of United Kingdom Energy Statistics*, London: Stationary Office.

Energy Information Administration (2001) *Electric Power Annual*, Washington: US Department of Energy.

International Energy Agency (2001) *Competition in Electricity Markets*, Paris: OECD/IEA.

International Energy Agency (2001) *Energy Policies of IEA Countries*, Paris: OECD/IEA.

International Energy Agency (2001) *Towards a Sustainable Energy Future*, Paris: OECD/IEA.

International Energy Agency (2001) *Energy Statistics of OECD Countries*, 1998-1999, Paris: OECD/IEA.

International Energy Agency (2001) *Energy Balances of OECD Countries*, 1998-1999, Paris: OECD/IEA.

International Energy Agency (2001) *IEA Statistics: Electricity Information 2001*, Paris: OECD/IEA.

International Energy Agency (1999) *Electricity Reform: Power Generation Costs and Investment*, Paris: OECD/IEA.

International Energy Agency (quarterly) *Energy Prices and Taxes*, Paris: OECD/IEA.

Monopolies and Mergers Commission (1996) *National Power and Southern Electric A report on the proposed merger*, CM 3230HMSO London SW8 5DT

Monopolies and Mergers Commission (1996) *PowerGen and Midlands Electricity plc: A report on the proposed merger*, CM 3231, HMSO London SW8 5DT

The National Grid Company plc (2001) *Seven Year Statement 2000/2001*, London: NGC.

Nordel (2000) *Annual Report*, Oslo.

Statistics Norway (2000) *Electricity Statistics*, Oslo.

ORDER FORM

IEA BOOKS

Fax: +33 (0)1 40 57 65 59
E-mail: books@iea.org
www.iea.org/books

INTERNATIONAL ENERGY AGENCY

9, rue de la Fédération
F-75739 Paris Cedex 15

I would like to order the following publications

PUBLICATIONS	ISBN	QTY	PRICE		TOTAL
☐ **Security of Supply in Electricity Markets - Evidence and Policy Issues**	**92-64-19805-9**		**US$100**	**€110**	
☐ Distributed Generation in Liberalised Electricity Markets	92-64-19802-4		US$75	€82	
☐ Competition in Electricity Markets	92-64-18559-3		US$75	€82	
☐ Regulatory Institutions in Liberalised Electricity Markets	92-64-18583-6		US$75	€82	
☐ Nuclear Power in the OECD	92-64-18579-8		US$60	€66	
☐ Electricity in India - Providing Power for the Millions	92-64-19724-9		US$125	€137	
☐ World Energy Outlook - 2001 Insights	92-64-19658-7		US$150	€165	
☐ Russia Energy Survey 2002	92-64-18732-4		US$150	€165	
			TOTAL		

DELIVERY DETAILS

Name ______ Organisation ______

Address ______

Country ______ Postcode ______

Telephone ______ E-mail ______

PAYMENT DETAILS

☐ I enclose a cheque payable to IEA Publications for the sum of US$ ______ or € ______

☐ Please debit my credit card (tick choice). ☐ Mastercard ☐ VISA ☐ American Express

Card no: ______

Expiry date: ______

Signature:

OECD PARIS CENTRE
Tel: (+33-01) 45 24 81 67
Fax: (+33-01) 49 10 42 76
E-mail: distribution@oecd.org

OECD BONN CENTRE
Tel: (+49-228) 959 12 15
Fax: (+49-228) 959 12 18
E-mail: bonn.contact@oecd.org

OECD MEXICO CENTRE
Tel: (+52-5) 280 12 09
Fax: (+52-5) 280 04 80
E-mail: mexico.contact@oecd.org

You can also send your order to your nearest OECD sales point or through the OECD online services: www.oecd.org/bookshop

OECD TOKYO CENTRE
Tel: (+81-3) 3586 2016
Fax: (+81-3) 3584 7929
E-mail: center@oecdtokyo.org

OECD WASHINGTON CENTER
Tel: (+1-202) 785-6323
Toll-free number for orders:
(+1-800) 456-6323
Fax: (+1-202) 785-0350
E-mail: washington.contact@oecd.org